50 GREAT FARMSTAYS IN NEW ZEALAND

50 GREAT FARMSTAYS IN NEW ZEALAND

Philip Holden

A personal tour with photographs and maps

Hodder Moa Beckett

Author's Note

All the farmstays featured in this book are included at my choice — rather than that of my publisher. The criteria I set for inclusion was that each one had to be a genuine working property rather than a life-style block.

Since the word 'station' is used frequently in this book, it is necessary to explain it for those unfamiliar with the term. 'Station' originally meant the actual place where runholders would base themselves to work their property. Later, the name came to mean the entire set-up: both land and stock. A station was normally a large block of land of Government or Maori leasehold land — usually both. The name station still applied if the property subsequently became freehold. There is no clear distinction between a station and farm but it is generally accepted that any property that has the capacity to carry between 2000 and 3000 sheep can be considered a station.

As a general guideline, accommodation rates for farmstays start at about $80 for a double room per night, including breakfast, but not dinner which is optional. A top level farmstay might cost up to $300 per room per night, including breakfast and a hosted three-course dinner with aperitifs and complimentary New Zealand wine. Single rooms are of course less expensive than doubles, as are other forms of accommodation offered on various farms and stations.

I would like to sincerely thank everyone included for allowing me to visit their homes in various parts of the country.

Philip Holden
Queenstown, 2000

Cover credits

Front Cover, clockwise from left:

Castlerock Cookhouse p.112
Kahutara Station p.64
Rarakau Station p.122
Glenview p.74
Tasman Downs Station p.82

Back Cover, top to bottom:

Ben Lomond p.20
Hiburn Station p.96
Tophouse p.62
Holbrook Station p.78

Title Page:

Shortlands Station p.92

ISBN 1-86958-818-5

© 2000 – Original text and photographs – Philip Holden
The moral rights of the author have been asserted

© 2000 Design and format – Hodder Moa Beckett Publishers Ltd

This edition published in 2000 by Hodder Moa Beckett Publishers Ltd
[a member of the Hodder Headline Group],
4 Whetu Place, Mairangi Bay, Auckland, New Zealand

Produced and designed by Hodder Moa Beckett Publishers Ltd

Colour separations by Microdot, Auckland
Printed by Toppan Printing Co., Hong Kong

Contents

Introduction

On a glorious summer's afternoon, I visited Walter Peak Station. It is located across Lake Wakatipu from Queenstown. With a camera bag slung over my shoulder, and wearing Levis, sneakers and a peaked cap, I might have been mistaken for a tourist from North America as the TSS *Earnslaw* sailed across the placid waters of the third largest lake in the land. Instead, I was locally based and it was my intention was to photograph the garden at the Walter Peak homestead and whatever else caught my eye.

While I was photographing, a typical group of tourists were being given a conducted tour of the immediate homestead area, a tour I had done in the previous autumn or fall. So I knew they would be told something of the station's colourful history, its size and what stock they ran. In the woolshed they would be shown how a sheep was shorn and they would get an opportunity to touch some tame sheep and docile highland cattle.

As the *Earnslaw* returned to Queenstown, I found myself engaged in conversation with a likeable couple from California. He was interested to know what kind of camera I was 'shooting with'. It turned out he was using a Nikon, a newer and more sophisticated model than my old F-301.

In any event, they had enjoyed their trip to Walter Peak but, the man added, it hadn't really been long enough to get a real grasp of farming practices. He went on to say they had another three weeks or so left in the country. They had a rental car and were staying at motels along the way. The problem with that, the woman added, was that they weren't getting to know any locals. Her husband nodded in agreement.

Well, at this time I had visited about 40 of the 50 farmstays included in the following pages. I told them about this project and then asked if they had ever considered staying at a farmstay. No, they hadn't, was their reply. I explained some more of the advantages of staying on a farm or station.

'Station?'

'Same thing as a ranch.' 'And the best thing of all', I went on, 'is that you'd really get to meet some locals that way.'

They were both enthusiastic at the idea, the man boyishly so. Could I recommend any such place? He asked. Recommend? I could recommend with the utmost confidence a whole bunch of farmstays for them to stay at! **Philip Holden**

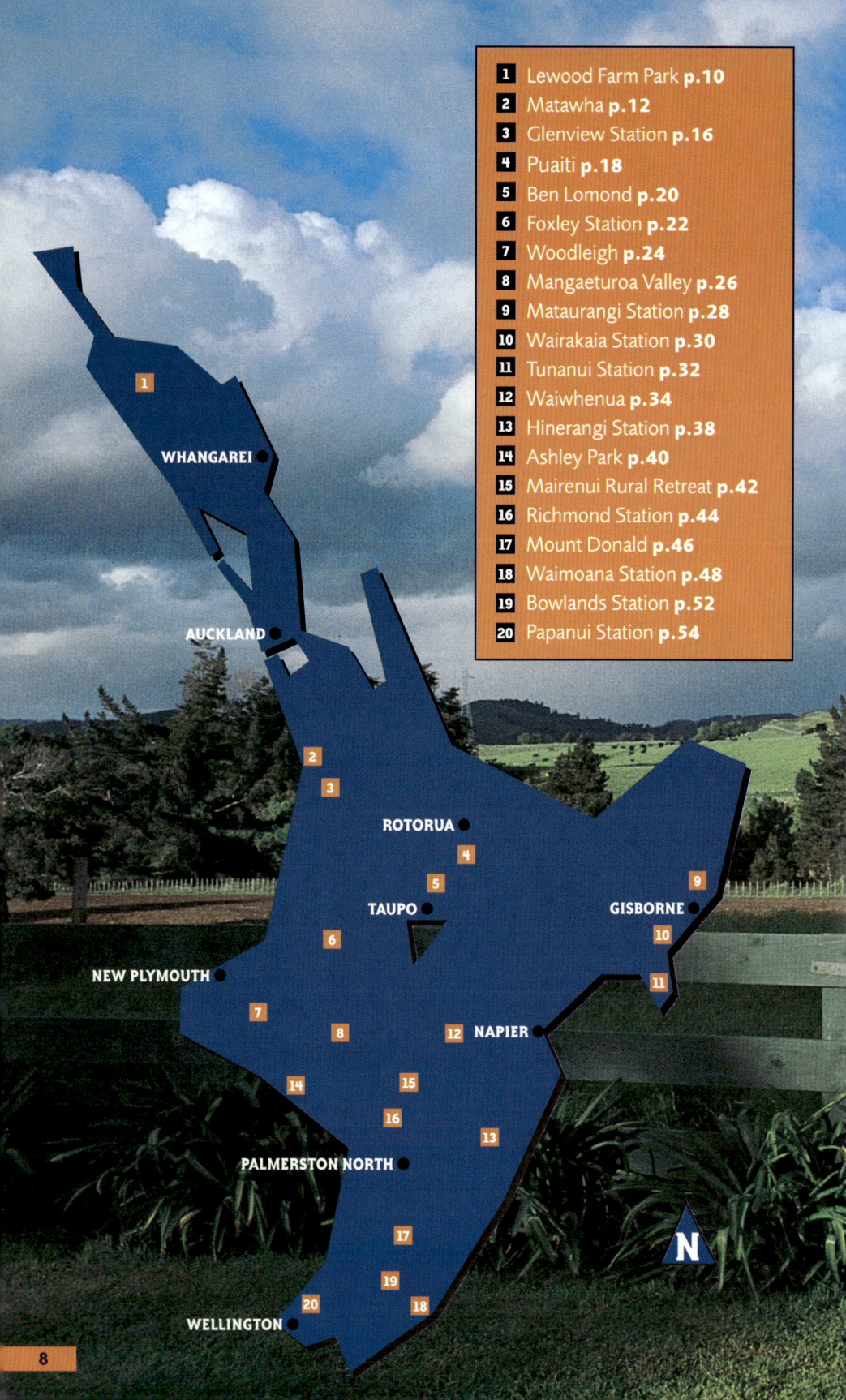

WHANGAREI

AUCKLAND

ROTORUA

TAUPO

GISBORNE

NEW PLYMOUTH

NAPIER

PALMERSTON NORTH

WELLINGTON

N

The North Island

Richmond Station, p. 44.

1 Lewood Farm Park

Hosts: Pat and Ron Lewis
Location: Okaihau, Bay of Islands
Address: Lewood Farm Park,
Mangataraire Road, RD1, Okaihau,
Bay of Islands
Phone: (09) 401-9290 or (09) 401-9941 or
(025) 277-7305

Fax: (09) 401-9290
Size: 404 hectares (1000 acres)
Stock: sheep, cattle, forestry
Accommodation: spacious farmhouse,
two bedrooms, one guest bathroom
Nearest town: Okaihau 15 minutes

The northernmost farmstay I visited was located at the head of the Mangataraire Valley, perhaps 15 minutes' drive out of Okaihau (on Highway 1). It was called Lewood Farm Park. To the best of my knowledge, it is the only property of a substantial size offering farmstay holidays in Northland.

Pat and Ron Lewis, your hosts, are a relaxed, pleasant and eager-to-please couple. Over coffee and cake, Ron explained that they were presently carrying over 1000 Romney cross-bred sheep and 120 Angus cross-bred cattle. There were also 'heaps of wild turkeys' on the place, he added wryly. No, he was not intending to farm them.

They had been doing farmstays for six years. At that time, with their three children grown up and elsewhere, Pat had recently finished working full time and she felt at a loose end. They were rather cut off here in a valley that did not receive electricity until 1947. Perhaps a sense of isolation prevailed. But once they started their farmstay business, and people from overseas, mainly from England, began to visit them — well, all that changed dramatically.

Presently we went off for a look at some of the buildings on the place. They had been here since the early 1900s, says Ron. He should know. His grandfather, Frederick, was one of three brothers who broke in the land.

The three Lewis boys, born in Waipu, were the sons of a Captain Lewis, master of the ship *Bredalbana*, which transported some of the pioneer settlers from Nova Scotia to New Zealand.

Working in the kauri forests around Dargaville, the boys became expert woodsmen. Much later, in 1896, they purchased 3000 acres of bush-clad hill country from the Crown. They named it Utakura. Today, Ron and his cousin, Ross, own adjoining farms and collectively they have about two-thirds of the original land holding.

The original homestead (now on Ross's property) was, explained Ron, made of kauri felled and pit-sawn here. The same thing could be said of the three-stand woolshed. However, a cottage dating back to the same period had been mostly built of totara. Those picturesque old buildings made me feel like I'd been transported back in time.

It gave me a kick to discover that Pat and Ron were breeders of blue heelers — one of my favourite breeds of dog. How had that started?

'A nephew of mine dropped off a pup here,' explained Ron, 'cause I'd admired his blue heeler; he was pighunting, you see. There were still wild pigs on the place. Pat thought it was the ugliest critter she'd ever seen but it grew on her. Then one day she surprised me by saying she'd like to breed them. There was a breeder at Marton with a couple of litters for sale and off we went.'

That day there were five blue heelers at Lewood Farm Park and they are registered breeders. Ron uses them alternatively for what they do best — work cattle.

While Lewood Farm Park might seem remote to some, it is only an easy drive to many of the attractions for which the Bay of Islands is famous. The farm could prove an ideal base for exploring this attractive part of the country known as the 'winterless north'.

Left: Ron and Pat's farmhouse is more spacious and well-appointed than it appears from the outside.
Top right: Ron and Pat, with Ruby and Sheila, two of the blue heelers.
Right: The glorious colours of spring.

2 Matawha

Host: Jenny Thomson
Location: Ruapuke
Address: Matawha, Raglan, No. 61 RD2
Phone: (07) 825-6709
Fax: (07) 825-6715
E-mail: jennyt@wave.co.nz

Size: 364 hectares (900 acres)
Stock: sheep, cattle
Accommodation: self-contained accommodation adjoining main farmhouse, one bedroom, private bathroom
Nearest town: Raglan 18 km

The sun was going down in a spectacular fashion on Matawha. The distinctive volcanic cone that is Mount Karioi was bathed in a pale orange glow. Some 15 km out to sea Gannet Island was brilliantly aglow. It had been named by Captain Cook in 1770 during his circumnavigation of the North Island because of the large numbers of gannets nesting there.

On the immediate headland between the farmhouse and the Tasman Sea were Romney sheep and cross-bred cattle.

The Thomson family have been here on Matawha since the mid-1880s. According to Jenny Thomson, a gold strike in the South Island was the reason William Thomson, a Scotsman, was able to purchase Matawha. Following his great fortune in Central Otago, he moved to the Gisborne area. While there he heard of a likely block of land for sale near Raglan. Saddling his horse, he set off to check it out, the ride taking three days. Liking what he saw of what was still mostly a bush block sweeping down to the sea, he purchased it.

A country girl from the Manawatu, Jenny was a nurse in her younger days. She also worked on a Murray Grey cattle stud in Melbourne, Australia for two years, preparing the lovable animals for shows and so on. Her love of cattle later took her on a cattle tour to the Bay of Islands and it was on this trip that she met her late husband, Peter. They had two sons, Simon and David.

Above: Beyond the cattle, the Matawha farmhouse and pale waters of the sea can be seen.
Right: Mount Karioi.

Until quite recently they ran between 1100 and 1300 Romney sheep here; Matawha, under Peter Thomson's guiding hand, was well-known for its top quality Romney sheep. With sheep numbers cut back drastically, it is Jenny's intention to concentrate on increasing cattle numbers. She also owns another big block of land on Mount Karioi itself; some of it is still in native timber, which they have no intention of cutting down. Their cattle grow fat on the cleared country below 'Shaky Mountain'.

Jenny and her sons have been doing farmstays for 11 years now. Jenny has found it an enjoyable experience. Apart from her love of cattle, she enjoys gardening and that is reflected in both the main farmhouse garden and the big vegetable garden.

I especially liked the accommodation at Matawha. In a spacious bedroom/sitting-room is a comfortable lounge suite, a television for people who don't want to switch off entirely, and everything else — tea, coffee, magazines and books — to make for an agreeable stay.

To wake up here and take in the panoramic view, which includes both Karioi and the sea, is a lovely and relaxing way to start a brand new day.

The mountain dominates this and other big farms in the area. There is an excellent walk to be had on the mountain, as the track is well-graded. People staying at Manawha can either drive (or be taken) to a nearby farm and leave their vehicles there to walk the mountain. The track takes you right to the top of Karioi.

A short drive away are the Te Mata Bridal Veil Falls, which are found in a bush reserve between Te Mata and Kawhia. The falls plunge a good 60 m into a deep pool. They are a must to see.

On the farm itself is a private beach. You like fishing? This is the spot. At times seals can be seen on the beach; they are thought to come here from Gannet Island. Also horseriding can be arranged. Again the farm is great for walking, the view always arresting no matter the weather. A group of local trampers had been walking on the farm when I arrived.

Left: Te Mata Bridal Veil Falls.
Below: The last of the sun spears across Gannet Island.

3 **Glenview Station**

Hosts: Cindy and Warren Clayton-Greene
Location: King Country
Address: Glenview Station, RD8, Te Kuiti
Phone: (07) 878-7705
Fax: (07) 878-5066
Size: 890 hectares (2200 acres)

Stock: sheep, cattle, horses
Accommodation: modern farmhouse dating to 1979, self-contained accommodation, two bedrooms, one en suite, lounge with television, etc.
Nearest town: Te Kuiti 23 km

This was essentially limestone country on Glenview Station: typically rough, broken terrain, bisected by many streams and made difficult by crumbling bluffs and craggy cliffs sweeping to around 365 m.

We probed deeper into a narrow valley contained by amazing cliffs. Suddenly, my attention was arrested by a big mob of multi-coloured wild goats climbing steadily to higher ground.

'Lots of them on the place,' remarked Warren Clayton-Greene matter-of-factly.

'Maybe you should farm them, too,' I suggested facetiously: it wasn't that long ago that feral goats were rounded up large-scale and farmed. They were seen as a possible salvation of a flagging farming industry. But the only ones that have time for wild goats these days are other wild goats. Warren didn't bother replying.

We jolted across a bridged stream where rainbow and brown trout lurked in deep pools. They were not easy to catch, Warren admitted.

In a light drizzle, and with the station's high country lost in mist, I noticed large numbers of Angus/Hereford cattle and some Romney sheep. Warren explained that they ran around 5000 sheep and 700 cattle.

Left: A section of the garden and conservatory of the homestead at Glenview Station.
Above: Cindy and Warren enjoy their life in the King Country backblocks.
Right: The tiny figures of Warren and Cindy are seen on the track near the woolshed and sheep yards complex.

'What about goats?'

This time I got a grunt in reply.

Warren's family (and brother, too) took on Glenview Station in 1977. Until then his parents had farmed north of Taupo, while he and his brother were working on East Coast stations.

In the early 1980s, Warren took time out to visit Canada. It was while working on a ranch owned by Cindy's sister and brother-in-law that he met the lady herself. In 1983 Cindy came out to New Zealand and, as she says, she wouldn't want to live anywhere else now.

While Cindy was born and raised in Idaho, her family, all from a ranching background, later moved to Canada.

'I'm one of five kids,' she says, 'and we all lived on ranches.' She grinned. 'I'm the only one over here.' Then: 'My family have been involved in tourism as well as raising cattle for many years and so I was brought up in the tourist industry.' By that, she meant a guest ranch, a North American counterpart of New Zealand farmstays. The young Clayton-Greenes would go into the farmstay business after their two children, Kirsty and Wess, were born.

In these tough times, Warren and Cindy work the station together. They use horses for hill country work. There are eight horses on the place; Warren had broken in seven of them. Basically he is a dying breed: a King Country station owner who still relies on horses.

Cindy says she enjoys the hard physical work that is necessary on the station and working with her dogs. Also, she does all of their bookwork, looks after two school-age children, tends a lovely garden, and handles the farmstay side of things.

I don't think you should visit Glenview without seeing those wonderful limestone rock formations and dense stands of native bush. A strenuous hike over some of their country is a fine way of working up a great appetite for the evening meal with the family (Kirsty and Wess are great kids!)

On the doorstep are the world-famous glow worm caves at Waitomo (5 km away) and the nearby black sand beaches of the West Coast, at Marokopa, are also worth taking in.

4 Puaiti

Hosts: Barb and Philip Hawken
Location: Waikite Valley, Rotorua
Address: Puaiti, 471 Puaiti Road, RD1, Rotorua
Phone: (07) 333-1540 or (025) 854-258
Fax: (07) 333-1501

E-mail: puaitifarmstay@hotmail.com
Size: 484 hectares (1200 acres)
Stock: sheep, cattle, deer
Accommodation: three guest bedrooms, one double room and two twin rooms
Nearest town: Rotorua

It is difficult to imagine when you visit Puaiti today that as recently as the late 1950s and early 1960s this hilly country, a mere 35 minutes' drive from Rotorua, was still unbroken: a veritable forest of tight-knit manuka scrubland, with the odd, scattered stand of rimu. It was the haunt of legions of wild pig and large numbers of red deer that drifted there from the nearby Paeroa Range. Yet that is what it was when Peter Hawken took on what was termed a 'development block' from the Government. The 1200-acre block was named from the prolific white flowers of the manuka in spring.

On a pleasant spring morning, with the sun soon to break free of a misty barrier, Peter's daughter-in-law, Barb, pointed from her superb garden to a nearby hillside. Back in 1977, she explained, it was still clad in manuka. At that time they had decided to go into farming deer. There

were deer on the hill and scattered about the farm. As a boy, Philip can recall seeing herds of red deer on their place. They were then classed as virtually worthless and a pest to get rid of.

'It was there that we captured our first deer,' Barb went on, still indicating the hillside. The deer caught there with the help of a helicopter operator started the foundation of a red deer herd, which today numbers 2000.

They also run 2000 cross-bred sheep. At one time, they carried 4500 of them, but then they also had another two men working on the place. These days Philip is very much a one-man band, and, because deer require less work than sheep, they intend to increase their deer numbers while cutting back on sheep.

The two-acre garden at Puaiti is a delightful surprise. They started it 17 years ago. Because of a powerful wind factor here, they began with a shelterbelt of willows, pines and gum trees. Once these had grown sufficiently tall they started on the inner garden. Now among the gardens is a warm, modern home and nearby is a tennis court.

With Philip heavily involved in running the farm, it is up to Barb to show people around. She usually does this in a four-wheel-drive vehicle. On most days they'll catch up with Philip and see what he's up to. Often he'll be working with the sheep and so he'll show them what his dogs are capable of — plenty, in a word.

Apart from Puaiti itself, there is a hot pool area, squash court, and a golf course in the Waikite Valley, all less than 15 minutes' drive away. The golf course, on the steep side, is aptly named the 'Goat Track', but on the day I drove by, sheep, rather than goats, were grazing on the fairways — though fortunately, not on the fenced-off greens! Trout fishing is also available. There are also the many attractions of Rotorua and Taupo — an hour's drive away — to enjoy.

Left: The Puaiti homestead.
Above right: Red deer now graze behind fences where there was once a forest of manuka scrubland.

Below: Looking out from the garden to the hillside where Philip Hawken captured Puaiti's first wild deer.

5 Ben Lomond

Hosts: Jack and Mary Weston
Location: Taupo
Address: Ben Lomond, 1434 Poihipi Road, RD1, Taupo
Phone: (07) 377-6033 or (025) 774-080
Fax: (07) 377-6033

E-mail: benlomond@xtra.co.nz
Size: 202 hectares (500 acres)
Stock: sheep, cattle
Accommodation: self-contained cottage, plus two bedrooms in main homestead
Nearest town: Taupo 15 km

It was arguably the best of times to be taken on a farm tour of Ben Lomond by Jack Weston, for his Romney ewes had recently given birth and so there was a distinct feeling that it was all happening on the now pleasant top-dressed pumice-land property west of Taupo.

In the early 1900s large-scale timber milling started in the forests north of Lake Taupo. Where Ben Lomond and other farms can be found today was considered one of the biggest and finest stands of forest anywhere in the land. The principal trees were totara and matai, both eagerly sought-after hardwoods. The fallen timber was taken by rail on a twice-weekly basis to Putaruru until the forests that had taken forever to mature were no longer, and the land itself — from a purely commercial point of view — was viewed altogether differently.

It is on Mary Weston's side of the family that their connection with today's Ben Lomond began. Her grandfather was JA Macfarlane. He was involved with McLean's famous station in Hawke's Bay, Maraekakaho. A man of some means, Macfarlane ventured to the country north of Lake Taupo and, according to Mary, '... was able to buy a lot of land up this way.'

The original block of which Ben Lomond is now a small part was 5000 acres in size. Macfarlane appears to have taken it on in the early 1930s and, rather than living there himself, he installed a manager. In 1939 Macfarlane died, leaving the property to Mary's mother and her two sisters. Mary's father, a solicitor, bought out his sisters-in-law and went ahead to develop the property further. Lacking practical farming knowledge himself, it wasn't until he hired Dick Weston as

manager that things started to pick up. Dick's son, Jack, has been running the place since 1960; later, he and Mary married.

At the time of my visit, on Ben Lomond they were running 1200 ewes — 'Never anything but Romneys here', says Jack Weston, and 160 Angus/Shorthorn breeding cows. There were also some horses on the place, a pet pig and a steer, and dogs that were very much a part of the family.

Given its close proximity to Taupo (less than 15 minutes' drive away), Ben Lomond is ideally situated for anyone wanting the relaxation of a pleasant farmstay but also wanting to enjoy what the region has to offer. The Taupo region, boasting the largest lake in the country, can be rightly regarded as the playground of the central North Island volcanic plateau. Basically whatever you feel inclined to do — fishing, playing golf, horse riding, enjoying flights over the mountains of National Park — hey, it's all here. Given their local knowledge and contacts, either Jack or Mary can point you in the right direction.

The garden at Ben Lomond looked a treat and so did its cottage accommodation. The cottage is fully self-contained, but people can still eat with Mary and Jack in the comfortable homestead if they wish. To judge by the smoked trout Mary served up one mealtime, I'd skip cooking for myself and make sure I was at the dining table in the main homestead when the main meal of the day was served up. Wine is included in the price for dinner, too.

Left: The self-contained cottage at Ben Lomond.
Above: In a light drizzle, this Romney ewe and her lambs are somewhat pensive.
Below: Jack Weston feeding his horses, Fancy the grey and a Dozen Roses. They came eagerly to his call.

6 Foxley Station

Hosts: Kitrena and Tony Fullerton-Smith
Location: King Country
Address: Foxley Station, RD, Ongarue
Phone: (07) 896-6104
Fax: (07) 896-6919

Size: 1616 hectares (3500 acres)
Stock: sheep, cattle, deer
Accommodation: spacious homestead, two bedrooms, one private bathroom
Nearest town: Taumarunui 25 km

The Foxley Station homestead, some of which dated to 1905, was set in delightful grounds. In front of the homestead a small herd of red deer, a fine stag in the velvet among them, were contained in a small paddock. Nearby was the house that the manager Tony 'Spud' Manning and his wife, Sandy, lived in. Then there were the woolshed, cookhouse, and shearers' quarters all dating to a much earlier period. The Ohura River flowed by those old buildings and then made a great loop so that it came close to the homestead. Trees such as totara and kowhai grew on the banks of the river.

The hills marched back to the skyline at the station's western boundary. Romney sheep and Angus cattle ranged over some of the hills where stands of native timber had been left. This was where Tony Fullerton-Smith, a husky character in his forties, has spent most of his life.

Tony's grandfather first took up the station in the late 1890s. It was then a typical King Country bush block contained in a valley and comprising about 8000 acres. Naturally clearing the land was the main order of the day. There was a big timber mill nearby in the 1920s and a lot of milling went on through the latter part of the decade and again in the late 1930s and early 1940s. By then Tony's grandfather had died and his son Sam, Tony's father, carried on. In 1989, Tony and his wife, Kitrena, purchased the main block of 4000 acres known as Foxley Station.

Situated on State Highway 40, Foxley Station is conveniently located midway between Auckland and Wellington. Wairarapa-born Kitrena says:

'We find that most people who stay with us really want to see how a station works. They like to look around the woolshed and actually touch wool.'

They also get a big kick out of seeing a sheep shorn, and also getting about the place as I did, on the back of Tony's seemingly go-anywhere farmbike. Normally they have no more than four people staying with them here — family groups or friends travelling together — and so with two such farmbikes to call on they can take out everyone at the same time. But as Kitrena pointed out, some of the women were happier walking if the country appeared steep.

While I was out with Tony, I'd noticed a big stand of native timber that was also situated on steep, hilly ground. It was now a native bush reserve, explained Tony. There was a track through it, he went on, and it was a particularly good spot to see and hear birds. As the bush reserve wasn't that far from the homestead they always suggested that their guests take advantage of it.

Over a dinner of wild game that night, I asked what would they suggest people see and do if they were staying with them for several days. Kitrena answered, telling me that local attractions include trout fishing or flights over the central volcanic plateau. People could drive

Above left: The Foxley Station homestead.
Bottom left: The Foxley Station homestead as seen from the deer paddock.
Above: The cookhouse (foreground) and shearers' quarters date to a much earlier period on the station.

to the National Park (less than an hour away). Cruises on the Wanganui River were also popular. At Taumarunui was one of the finest golf courses in the country.

But if I were to stay at Foxley for a few days, well, I'd be content to take advantage of what the station itself has to offer: make the most of the fine homestead, stroll about the beautiful gardens that have taken over 20 years to develop to their present stage. Then I might take a swim if the weather was suitable or head off to the bush reserve and watch and listen to the birds. Certainly I'd take a lot of photographs.

7 Woodleigh

Hosts: Heather and Peter Savage
Location: Taranaki
Address: Woodleigh, Toko Road, RD22,
Stratford
Phone: (06) 762-2840 or (025) 284-3820
Fax: (06) 762-2880
E-mail: savage.toko@xtra.co.nz
Size: 464 hectares (1150 acres)
Stock: sheep, dairy cattle
Accommodation: modern farmhouse, one
double bedroom, one en suite
Nearest town: Stratford 17 km

I would discover that on Woodleigh, they were very much into self-sufficiency — far more than in any other place I had yet been. By that, I mean that Peter Savage had installed a water-wheel down at the nearby creek. It generated enough power to provide all of the electrical needs not only for their home but also for the house their married share-milker resided in. Moreover, Heather Savage had two big vegetable gardens which would, I thought, grow enough produce to supply a fair-sized supermarket on a regular basis. Ready for picking at the time of my visit were cabbages, strawberries, broccoli, lettuce, and radishes. Potatoes, corn, pumpkins, etc. would soon be ready to harvest. In addition, she made butter from the milk their cows produced and free-range hens provided eggs. She also ground wheat to make flour for her bread, which was delicious. It was very much like a Kiwi version of 'The Good Life'! After digesting all of this information in their roomy kitchen, I couldn't help but ask were they preparing for a worldwide disaster? They both laughed, Heather most of all.

Peter's great-grandfather, Thomas Bayley, took up about 12,000 acres of forest-clad land here in 1885. Within a year of doing so, he had transferred the lease to his son, Charles, who faced the daunting task of breaking it in.

By the late 1920s the property, due to the inevitable subdivision, was reduced to about a quarter of its original size. When Charles died in 1939, the property passed on to Peter's mother and an uncle.

Wellington-born Peter would spend many a holiday on the family farm in Taranaki. From it were wonderful views of the mountain — then known as Egmont but now as Taranaki.

The farm was split among family members in 1993 and Peter found himself the owner of 1150 acres of hill country farm. Today, he runs 850 Romney sheep and 200 dairy cattle (they are currently milking 410 cows twice daily). His long-term intention was to phase out sheep altogether. Also, he plants 10 acres a year in trees, and as a result, now has about 100 acres in pine trees.

Heather is also from the city. So how had an Auckland girl adapted to life in the country? She laughed at that and said that her parents initially thought she was going to the ends of the earth but now thought otherwise — indeed, they often came to the farm to visit.

But she had found the more relaxed way of life to her liking. She admits that she is not as involved with the running of the farm as most farmers' wives are. But that's all right. There's plenty to keep her busy. She has two school-age children — Robert, 13, and Nicola, 10 — to look after. Then there are the vegetable gardens, the homestead garden, hens, pet lambs (two at the present time) and she also works as a relief teacher at Toko school.

Both Peter and Heather love the sea. They have a boat and take regular trips to the Bay of Islands, where they might camp out for up to three weeks at a time. They go fishing, sailing, water skiing and scuba diving. It was all a great contrast to life on the farm.

Most of the people who stay with them would rather savour 'life on the farm' than go further afield — which, in essence, is what farmstays are all about. Indeed, people here have every opportunity to join in with farm activities. I'm sure that Heather would have no objections to anyone offering to weed her vegetable gardens — providing they could find a weed, that is!

Having said that, however, Woodleigh would also be an ideal base in the country for anyone wanting to make the most of what Egmont National Park has to offer: skiing, hiking, nature walks, etc. The Pioneer Village at nearby Stratford is well worth a visit, too. But I'll bet you'll remember staying on Woodleigh more than anything else, as Peter and Heather are a really lovely couple.

Left: Part of the Woodleigh farmhouse, its garden and the hill beyond it.
Above: A break in the rain allowed me to photograph Peter and Heather.
Below: Looking out from the front garden to dairy cattle grazing on a nearby hillside.

8 Mangaeturoa Valley

Hosts: Ken and Sonia Robb
Location: Raetihi
Address: Mangaeturoa Valley, Ken and Sonia Robb, Pipiriki Road, Raetihi RD4
Phone: (06) 385-4581
Fax: (06) 385-4581
E-mail: ken.sonia@xtra.co.nz

Size: 404 hectares (1000 acres)
Stock: sheep, cattle
Accommodation: comfortable home, two guest bedrooms, one en suite, one share bathroom
Nearest town: Raetihi 6 km

Apart from the persistent rain that was dogging my progress through the western side of the North Island, I suppose that I really couldn't have chosen a better time to visit Ken and Sonia Robb's farm near Raetihi than when I did. Not only was the country looking good because so much of the wet stuff had recently fallen but their garden was a visual treat, too. Also, in a nearby paddock, were two 'pet' Romney lambs, several lovely Simmental calves, and three little black pigs which, in their own piggy way, were just as lovely. Apparently lost, they had been brought back to the nerve centre of the farm by Ken in the middle of a mob of sheep. While born wild, there was nothing of that about them now.

Over afternoon tea and cakes, Sonia told me that one of the lambs was named Helpful.

He had been named that by one of her granddaughters. At the time Sonia was pegging out the washing and the lamb was playing around the clothes basket and, the way the little girl saw it, was being 'helpful'. Sonia had other ideas about it.

When Fred Robb took on the 1000-acre property in 1941 it was an established farm; the land had been mostly cleared of all valuable timber though there is still a stand of native forest on the place. Today his son, Ken, runs around 1800 Romney sheep and close to 100 Simmental cows; establishing a Simmental stud in 1983.

They started their farm tours in 1987.

From the farmhouse garden there are fine views of Mount Ruapehu and, from a high point on the property, almost all of the western side of Tongariro National Park can be seen. The garden area itself attracts many native birds such as tui, bellbirds and fantails and I also had a great time with the young animals there.

Local attractions of course include the national park, with its excellent skifields and hiking tracks. Close, too, is Pipiriki (40 minutes' drive), on the banks of the Wanganui River. Wanganui itself is about 90 minutes' drive via State Highway 4.

Left: The Robbs' farmhouse.
Above: Even in gloomy conditions the garden looked a treat.
Right: Simmental calves; this breed is noted for its calm temperament.

9 Mataurangi Station

Host: Nick Reed
Location: East Coast
Address: Mataurangi Station, Panikau Road, Whangara
Phone: (06) 862-2858
Fax: (06) 862-2857
E-mail: mataurangi@xtra.co.nz
Size: 607 hectares (1482 acres)
Stock: sheep, cattle, horses
Accommodation: self-contained cottage that sleeps three, one double and one single bed. Dinner also available.
Nearest town: Gisborne 50 km

There was considerable movement at the station when I arrived at Matauarangi in the high country of the East Coast. The host was working with his sheep in the four-stand woolshed that dates to the early 1950s. Nick was both tall and tanned and the Romney sheep in the shed and in the yards appeared in good health, too.

'I've near done here,' said Nick, his educated voice seemingly at odds with the grimy working clothing he wore so easily. 'Take a look at the cottage in the meantime if you like. It's through that gate over there.'

The self-contained cottage — located within a couple of minutes' walk from the main homestead but offering complete privacy — is called The Roost. The word 'roost' can mean 'a perch upon which birds rest at night' or 'a place offering temporary sleeping accommodation'.

When I checked out The Roost, a tui was feeding on the nectar of a flax bush close by, a couple of native pigeons swept overhead and a fantail was showing off near the verandah. From the verandah the view was of sweeping country — sheep, cattle, and horses grazing — and I could have cheerfully stayed here a

couple of nights. As it was, I would be staying with my host at his place.

Matauarangi was originally a part of Panikau station, says Nick Reed. Nick's great-grandfather, Edward, took up that 9000-acre block in 1884. Panikau was subdivided among family members in 1946.

These days, he winters 1300 Romney ewes and 375 replacement ewe hoggets and he produces 10,000 kg of wool and 1400 lambs. There are also 185 Hereford cross-bred cattle on the place and a few horses that are used for mustering. Mostly, however, he uses four-wheel-drive farmbikes to get around the country as much of it is on the steep side. Also, he has planted radiata pine on some of the less productive hill country, to stabilise it. When Nick was growing up, his father employed three men on the place and there were often gangs of scrubcutters and fencers to feed, too. These days he works the place alone — not easy, but there it is.

Nick suggests that his guests plan to stay here at least two nights (some might stay for a week). I'd go along with that line of thought: the station is an hour's drive from Gisborne and there is simply so much to see and enjoy that you should give yourself at least one full day on the place. Also, the famous Panikau Gardens, located at the 'homestead block' of the original station, are nearby. They are a must to visit.

The drive from Gisborne to the station is an enjoyable one, following the wonderful coastline to Whangara and then heading inland on Panikau Road. This winding inland route follows the tops of ridges so that the country falls away and the views are extended. While it's only 23 km from Whangara to the station it seems longer than this. Indeed, I was starting to think I had overshot the mark, when there on my left was a mailbox and a sign saying I'd reached my destination. From this point it is an awesome view: a long driveway descends down to the station, wild bushlands abound, and there is Mount Hikurangi on the skyline.

Left: A perfect place to get away – the self-contained cottage, The Roost.
Right: Mount Hikurangi is the highest point on the East Coast.
Below: It was a busy time at the woolshed when I arrived at Mataurangi.

10 Wairakaia Station

Hosts: Rodney and Sarah Faulkner
Location: Muriwai, East Coast
Address: Wairakaia Station, 1894 State Highway 2, Gisborne RD2
Phone: (06) 862-8607 or Free phone: 0800 329-060
Fax: (06) 862-8607

E-mail: wairakaia@xtra.co.nz
Size: 646 hectares (1600 acres)
Stock: sheep, cattle
Accommodation: gracious homestead dating to 1905, three guest bedrooms, one en suite, one guest bathroom
Nearest town: Gisborne 25 km

The woodland garden at Wairakaia, a mere 2 km from the coast, was looking at its best on a wonderful spring day when the temperature nudged the mid-20s. Indeed, the moment you turn off State Highway 2 and follow a long, tree-lined drive up to the homestead area you are in for a visual treat. Most of the established trees here were planted in the early 1900s by Albert Faulkner, the grandfather of present-day owner, Rodney. Among the trees were two prolific avocados, a pear, and fine 'exotic' specimens from the 'old country' flanking the driveway. In season, a veritable riot of daffodils creates a brilliant yellow carpet below those same trees.

I strolled up from the homestead with Sarah Faulkner, past the sunken tennis court, and came to a wooded area before descending to the garden proper with its magnolias, camellias, and michelia, all in spring bloom. Here, too, were two goldfish ponds crossed by rustic bridges and the heady air was alive with the song of native birds, most of which were year-round residents.

Above: The homestead at Wairakaia dates to 1905.
Right: The old stables are a tangible link with a different era.
Left: Looking down from the homestead area to the old stables.

Later, in summer, their busiest time for guests to stay, Sarah's old roses — a bed of 50 'Margaret Merril' and 'Iceberg' — would reveal their beauty. At that time, cool breezes would sweep in from the nearby coast. And when winter arrived the garden was not prone to frost. 'We live in paradise, y'know,' Rodney Faulkner would say to me later.

Once again I had found myself on a farmstay with an interesting history. Prior to the arrival of the European, the land here at Muriwai at the southern end of Poverty Bay was favoured by Maori. On Wairakaia itself, there are obvious signs of Maori occupation: a fortified pa on high ground, kumara pits where they stored sweet potato, vegetable gardens, and burial grounds. Maori artefacts such as stone weapons have been found on the property. It is perhaps the highlight of Rodney's farm tour when he takes you up the valley of the Wairakaia Stream to visit this place. Time seems to stand still then as past and present collide.

Around the 1870s, an Englishman, John Woodbine Johnson, arrived on the scene with his brother, George. John had big ambitions. Soon he had established cordial relations with the local Maori. More than that, he married Mere Hape, a Maori woman of high birth whose family held title to land here. It did not take John long to take advantage of that to the tune of 11,000 acres of 'leasehold' land.

Over a period of 20 years, John gradually acquired the freehold rights for all of the property. When he died in the late 1890s the station was split up. Along came Albert Faulkner who snapped up the homestead block of about 3200 acres. Leaping ahead, the property was further reduced in 1950 when it was divided between Rodney's father and brother.

At present, they run a base flock of 2500 Coopworth ewes and 180 Hereford cows. There is also a forestry plantation on the property. Sarah and Rodney have travelled widely and are easy company. When Sarah can find the time she enjoys spinning. For his part, Rodney likes woodworking. Fortunately they both enjoy working in the garden — at one time, there would have been a least one person on the payroll as a full-time gardener. A farmstay here comes complete with a dog and two cats. Given that it is so close to Gisborne, this is a great place to base yourself and enjoy the many local attractions such as fine surf beaches and top wineries.

11 Tunanui Station

Hosts: Leslie and Ray Thompson
Location: Mahia, Northern Hawke's Bay
Address: Tunanui Station, Tunanui Road, RD8, Opoutama–Mahia
Phone: (06) 837-5790 or (025) 240-2421
Fax: (06) 837-5797
E-mail: tunanui@xtra.co.nz

Size: 1292 hectares (3200 acres)
Stock: sheep, cattle, goats, horses
Accommodation: fine self-contained accommodation: The Cottage — three bedrooms; The Farmhouse — four bedrooms
Nearest town: Wairoa 50 km

'The stars are crystal-clear, and the sunrise is an inspiring event,' says Leslie Thompson of Tunanui Station near Mahia on the sun-drenched East Coast. For when I returned to my accommodation for the night — a secluded cottage — the stars were clearly etched and seemingly only just out of my reach while at sunrise, I gazed out to sea and watched the sun rise over the Pacific Ocean, and might have been a pagan tribesman about to worship a tangible god.

As I drove back to the Thompsons' homestead for breakfast I was struck by the stunning view of their hill country property. It was still early and, in the early morning light, the ridges and spurs were knife-edged and stock — sheep, cattle, and even goats — were everywhere. More, I was able to see much of the arresting Mahia Peninsula; the sea sparkling about it.

According to Ray, Tunanui started off as a small bush block in 1912, when his grandfather, Fred, took it on. The trees were mainly tawa, kowhai and some rimu. Fred cleared enough land to build a home and run some dairy cattle. Every penny counted then — to help supplement their income, Ray's grandmother made butter and took her produce by horseback three miles to the local store.

In 1963, Ray joined his father, Horace, on the block. It was still heavily clad in forest. In the years that followed they cleared it and, also, snapped up the adjoining land so that eventually Tunanui was of considerable size for the region. Today, they run 1600 Romney/Perendale sheep, about 2000 cross-bred cattle and up to 1500 goats. They also have an 800-acre block on the Mahia Peninsula where they take cattle to fatten them up.

The goats interested me. Ray explained that they had been used to control blackberry for many years.

While Ray has lived at Tunanui for all of his life, Leslie came to what she describes as 'this remote and beautiful spot' as a young bride. They worked together on the station. When their children, Angus and Aimee, went to school, so did Leslie as she took advantage of her home science and teaching diplomas.

They got into the farmstay business by meeting tourists while driving stock on the road. Being the friendly soul he is, Ray would invite them back to the homestead that his father had built and Leslie, as gregarious as her husband, would offer them home-made scones and tea. Often the tourists would stay the night in a cottage built for single shepherds named the Whare (hut). In 1991 they gave it a fresh coat of paint and soon they were inviting people to stay with them as paying guests. The cottage I would stay in was restored in 1995. Situated near the woolshed, it sits snugly among exotic trees near a four-hectare stand of native bush. Later, they would develop a larger dwelling, The Farmhouse, which also offers

Above left: The Cottage is another of those wonderful places to get away from it all.
Below left: Ray feeding two calves at once, a typical chore in the spring.
Above: Looking out from The Farmhouse to the Mahia Peninsula.

complete privacy and a spectacular view of the Mahia Peninsula.

Both forms of accommodation here are fully self-contained but dinner and drinks can be had with Ray and Leslie at their homestead and continental breakfasts are also available if required. Leslie is a top cook who chooses local produce such as the freshest fruit and salad vegetables, asparagus and whitebait seasoned with her own herbs. The local waters are alive with crayfish, snapper and shellfish. The station produces its own delicious lamb and beef.

Leslie, who serves on the New Zealand Rural Tourism Council, says there is much to do in the area: their guests can visit the Morere hot pools, stroll along the lovely beaches, explore caves, visit a local marae, enjoy deep-sea fishing, surf or play golf.

While on the station itself they can see what Ray's up to as he carries out the stock work on horseback.

12 Waiwhenua

Hosts: David and Kirsty Hill
Location: Hawke's Bay
Address: Waiwhenua, 808 River Road, RD9, Hastings, Hawke's Bay
Phone: (06) 874-2435 or (025) 759-369 or Free phone: 0800 HILLFARM (445-5376)
Fax: (06) 874-2465
E-mail: kirsty.hill@xtra.co.nz
Size: 404 hectares (1079 acres)

Stock: sheep, cattle, deer. With orchard
Accommodation: two guest bedrooms in historic homestead, share bathroom Campervans welcome. Backpacker accommodation (old station hut) also available
Nearest town: Napier/Hastings, both 50 km

In the early spring morning, I stood on the broad balcony of a two-storey homestead and looked towards the sun-hazed Kaweka Mountains. A profusion of native trees was spread out before me, the garden looked wonderful, and birdsong filled the clear air at an altitude of 185 m. Indeed, a fantail — cheep-cheeping — constantly flittered about me and I thought that was indeed a good omen for the rest of my time at Waiwhenua.

Waiwhenua is run by David and Kirsty Hill — a young, progressive couple with three children of primary school age: Robbie, William, and Amanda. Becky, their fox terrier, is also an integral part of the family.

Waiwhenua has an interesting history and that always adds to the overall appeal of any place. It was once a part of the 11,000-acre

Waikonini Block, which in itself was a part of Tunanui Station. Tunanui was taken up in 1861 by Captain Andrew Hamilton Russell. It consisted of over 30,000 acres of (originally) fern and swamp lands adjacent to the Tutaekuri River. Within a few years they were running up to 9000 sheep. At that time, shepherds were provided with tea, flour, and other basic foodstuffs. The workforce must have been considerable because they were allowed to kill as many as three sheep a day.

In 1874 the Waikonini Block was sold; later, Arthur Sheild purchased it. The Waikonini Hotel, a vital link on the Cobb & Co. stagecoach run from Napier to Taihape, was relocated and later became the station homestead.

Following the First World War, Waiwhenua was sub-divided into blocks of around 300 to 400 hectares, the Sheild family retained the homestead block, considered the best land in the district.

About 1960, Kirsty's father, Lindsay Smith, was taken on by John Sheild as manager. Lindsay and Susan Smith went on to purchase the station in 1972. David and Kirsty took over the property from her parents in 1993.

The Hills currently run 2000 Romney ewes, 600 mixed cattle, and 600–700 red deer. David thinks that with lambs, calves and fawns all putting in a recent appearance the total stock units have swelled to around 6000.

The 30-acre orchard was established in 1973 by Kirsty's father. He is considered the pioneer of kiwi fruit in Hawke's Bay, but kiwi fruit has been dispensed with and now they only grow apples and pears organically.

Given its inland location, Waiwhenua, says Kirsty, has to stand on its own merits rather

Left: The Waiwhenua homestead was once a hotel on the Cobb & Co. stagecoach run between Napier and Taihape.
Below: The woolshed here is one of the oldest in the district.

than, say, being a base for what can be termed local attractions. Having said that, Hastings and Napier are only 45 minutes' drive away and the village of Taradale even closer. As a matter of interest, people without transport can be picked up or dropped off at Taradale.

I suggest you stay at Waiwhenua two nights, which allows one full day on the place. The property is worth looking over with David in his four-wheel-drive vehicle. The country sweeping down to the river is especially lovely and there are top views of the Kaweka and Ruahine Ranges.

On my farm tour, I saw that the stock were in great shape. David estimated that some of the three-month-old calves were weighing up to 120 kg as a bunch of them and their mums watched us with great interest. I also saw heaps of pheasants and native birds. There's always the chance of seeing wild deer, too. It was also interesting to poke about in the six-stand woolshed, which is regarded as among the oldest in the district.

I found the Hills to be a charming family.

Kirsty's main hobby is her garden and using her computer — naturally, with such skills she does all their bookwork. Both she and David have been overseas; David, a top shearer, has shorn sheep in Australia and Britain.

But perhaps the most delightful touch to my entire Waiwhenua experience happened on the morning I left the place. While driving along River Road (a section of the old stagecoach route), I looked towards the Kaweka Mountains and it was impossible for me not to recall a time when I had hunted deer for a living there. It was then that I spotted some deer grazing on a narrow strip of grass adjacent to a stand of pine trees. I stopped to grab a quick photograph before they vanished in single file into the trees.

Above: The Hill family: Robbie (holding Becky), Amanda on dad's knee, Kirsty and William.
Right: An unexpected sight as I left Waiwhenua — wild deer!

13 Hinerangi Station

Hosts: Caroline and Dan von Dadelszen
Location: Central Hawke's Bay
Address: Hinerangi Station, RD1, Waipukurau
Phone: (06) 855-8273
Fax: (06) 855-8273
E-mail: carovond@amcom.co.nz

Size: 727 hectares (1800 acres)
Stock: sheep, cattle, deer
Accommodation: splendid homestead, two bedrooms, one queen-sized room and one twin room, guests share bathroom
Nearest town: Waipukurau 20 km

Hinerangi Station has a great deal going for it: attractive Hawke's Bay hill country offering panoramic views of the Ruahine Range, a grand homestead dating to 1920, and a stirring history of a time when stations, like many a homestead still in use, were on a grand scale.

All of this was going through my mind on a windy but otherwise fine spring evening as, along with Dan von Dadelszen and his son, Sam, 26, I found myself overlooking some of their back country. Here, some of their 5500 sheep, essentially a Romney-based flock, grazed on vividly green pastures. They also ran 450 cross-bred cattle and 600 red deer. With an explosion of new life on the place — lambs, calves and fawns — they were 'flat out' busy on Hinerangi.

Hinerangi was once a part of Woburn

Station. Woburn was taken up by a Scotsman, Purvis Russell, in 1851. The original flock of Merinos was landed at Mana Island, ferried ashore, and then brought to Hawke's Bay via the Wairarapa coastline and old Maori trails to their eventual destination.

By 1873 the flock stood at 21,306 sheep and Woburn, now increased in size, was close to 28,000 acres. But in 1901 the then Labour Government took over the property and subdivided it into 57 farms. It was then that Dan's grandfather drew the block in a ballot.

Set among lovely grounds, the Hinerangi homestead alone is worth visiting; the full-sized billiard room is especially arresting. When Caroline von Dadelszen showed me around it, she told me that it was designed by the architect Louis Hay. Caroline explained that

Hay played a large part in the re-building of Napier following the 1931 earthquake and that he was responsible for the now famous art deco aspect of many of the impressive buildings that can still be seen in Napier. Hay also built homesteads in Hawke's Bay and in the Gisborne district.

While Dan von Dadelszen has lived on Hinerangi since he was seven (he spent his earliest years on a nearby property), Caroline comes from Christchurch, where she trained to be a kindergarten teacher. Later, she applied for a position in Waipukarau and it was there that she met her future husband.

My accommodation at Hinerangi was a large, spacious room complete with a double bed and tea and coffee making facilities. It is situated (as is the other guest room) in a separate wing of the homestead. Privacy is assured due to its size and guests have a private entrance to come and go as they please.

There is also a swimming pool and a tennis court in Hinerangi's grounds and there are great walks to be had on the place. Dan von Dadelszen offers an interesting and informative farm tour, while their son Sam works full time on the place.

Both Dan and Caroline like to travel and they are interesting to talk to. Caroline is a great-granddaughter of Joseph Ward, the New Zealand Prime Minister between 1906–12 and 1928–30.

Caroline tells me that the nearby Tukituki River offers fine fly fishing. There are two good golf courses within 10 km. Some excellent East Coast beaches are less than an hour's drive away, as is Napier for that matter. So you won't get bored if you decide to spend a few days.

Left: A section of the Hinerangi homestead — the guest entrance is to the left and the guest wing (shaded) is to the right.
Above: Some of the pleasant 'wooded' garden where sheep graze and daffodils flower.
Below: Out on the station's high back country are Dan (left) and Sam. The huntaway (right) is in full voice.

14 Ashley Park

Hosts: Wendy Bowman and Barry Pearce
Location: Southern Taranaki
Address: Ashley Park, PO Box 36,
Waitotara, Wanganui
Phone: (06) 346-5917
Fax: (06) 346-5861
E-mail: ashley_park@xtra.co.nz
Size: 202 hectares (500 acres)

Stock: sheep, cattle
Accommodation: grand homestead, three guest bedrooms; one en suite. Also two fully-equipped motels, several cabins, a self-contained unit; power points for caravans and campervans (with full facilities)
Nearest town: Wanganui 29 km

Ashley Park was a most attractive setting with its small lake or large pond in the middle of a miniature forest of exotic and native trees and a profusion of flowering shrubs. Given that the spring morning was fine but cool, one might have been visiting a country estate in the south of England rather than a property in Taranaki.

It was a place to linger, as on the water were Canada geese, a coot, a few scaup, some mallards and a pair of graceful swans that might have been elegant black sailboats.

Then I strolled up from the area of the lake via a linking network of well-tended pathways to join Barry Pearce and a local, Katherine Goldsbury, as they went about their morning business.

At this particular time they were making the

rounds of various animals kept in grounds adjacent to the main homestead area. It was like a zoological garden, with its alpaca, donkeys, feral and kune kune pigs, goats, red and fallow deer, and various breeds of cattle. Nearby were 30 aviaries, alive with exotic birds.

So, too, was an antique and craft shop handily placed to the main road and, of course, the homestead. Wendy Bowman (Barry's wife) is interested in antiques and this was her brainchild. The shop, she says, is open daily from nine to five and they serve Devonshire teas there.

It was a distant cry from the days when an Englishman, George Pearce, took the property on about the turn of the 20th century. He became well-known for his stud sheep. The family also had another property of 6500 acres near Raetihi, which Barry's father, Cedric, ran until he came to Ashley Park about 1930. Barry has spent all of his life here, and took over the running of the place in 1955. Two years before this they built what was really stage one of the present homestead. The second storey was added in 1972. Seen from the road it has the look of a much earlier building.

While Ashley Park offers a wide variety of accommodation (the decks of their two motels look out over the lake), the main guest room in the homestead, with en suite, is charming. But then, charm is a word you could associate not only with the entire downstairs area of the homestead, to which guests have full access, but also with Barry and Wendy, too.

I especially liked their fine collection of paintings which grace the drawing room; but, most of all, I loved Barry's library, not just for his extensive collection of books but also for its old-world charm.

There is lots to do at Ashley Park. Pony rides are available and so, too, are an 18-hole mini golf course, croquet and petanque facilities, a swimming pool and a tennis court.

There is a woolshed available for barn dances and parties of up to 300 people and there is a farm airstrip for small planes to use.

Local attractions include the scenic Waitotara Valley, Waverley, Wanganui, Hawera and Mount Taranaki — all within one and a half hours' drive.

Ashley Park adjoins Barry's brother's property. Here, on 7000 acres, Jock Pearce has a big operation. Under the title 'Longview Partnership', they run 1250 dairy cows, 5000 Romney/Coopworth sheep, 750 Angus/Hereford cattle, and soon they would also be fattening 1000 bullocks. Barry has full access to Jock's place, and he prefers to take their guests for a good look around Jock's property as it is perhaps the only real station-sized property in these parts.

Left: The Ashley Park homestead is as grand as it appears from the garden in the early morning.
Below: Katherine feeding three calves, Buster the Belted Galloway, is between two Highland cattle.

15 Mairenui Rural Retreat

Hosts: Sue, David and Matt Sweet
Location: Rangitikei
Address: Mairenui Rural Retreat, Ruahine Road, Mangaweka 5456
Phone: (06) 382-5564 or (025) 517-545
Fax: (06) 382-5885
E-mail: mairenui@xtra.co.nz
Size: 320 hectares (760 acres)
Stock: sheep, cattle, horses
Accommodation: The Homestead — two bedrooms both with en suites; The Retreat — sleeps six in three bedrooms, share bathroom; The Colonial Villa — sleeps 10 in five bedrooms, two share bathrooms
Nearest town: Mangaweka 12 km

Because I once lived in Mangaweka, and nostalgia runs as deep there for me as the waters of the nearby Rangitikei River, it was a pleasure for me to pass through the tiny township en route to an idyllic rural retreat known as Mairenui.

Mairenui has been in David Sweet's family since 1906 and he is the third generation on the place. The property itself, however, was established in the late 1890s.

On this steep hill country fronting the Ruahine Ranges, David, Sue and their son, Matt, run around 1000 Romney sheep and 80 head of Hereford/Angus beef cattle, for they, as David says, 'do best in this type of country'. Indeed, the nature of the terrain, quite precipitous in some places, means he has to rely on horses, rather than farmbikes to do the stock work. No worries there, David reckons.

What I found especially interesting about the set-up here is that they've tackled it with unbridled enthusiasm. In short, what you get at Mairenui is an expertly organised rural experience which not only caters for small numbers of people but can, if the situation dictates, provide an ideal location for larger groups of people who may use it for conventions, etc.

Quite apart from The Homestead (the family home), guests who stay here have a choice of accommodation. The Retreat, for instance, was designed by architect, John Comeskey. It was built in the 1970s using timber milled on the property. This dwelling is surrounded by a miniature native forest and, among the trees on display, one can see rimu, matai, miro, and kahikatea. With a lovely garden, featuring roses, camellias, and rhododendrons, Sue sees The Retreat as a sort of romantic hideaway, for honeymooners or for two or three couples wanting a quiet weekend away from it all.

In complete contrast to The Retreat is The Colonial Villa, which dates to about 1895. Keeping it as original as possible, but including modern-day conveniences, it was restored by David and Matt in 1995. It, too, offers perfect privacy. I loved the furnishings from a bygone era that grace the many rooms, the open fireplaces, and the long and deep bath. The imposing verandahs are a lovely touch, too. With sweeping views from its large lawns, a country holiday here could be compared to a pleasant step back to an altogether different and more relaxing time.

The seminar room at Mairenui, which can hold 14 people, is a pit-sawn totara cottage that most likely predates the restored villa (the original homestead).

In summing up what they offer, Sue says: 'We offer a wide variety of on-site activities, such as tennis, croquet, petanque, bush walks, river swimming and fishing. There is an all-weather concrete tennis court and the petanque court is full-sized. David offers tours of the farm in a fully-restored 1953 Landrover, or a lift down to the river to fish or swim in our private pools — a real plus, that one. With one of the few privately owned stretches of river, catch-and-release brown trout fishing is available solely for our guests.

'Apart from everything the farm offers, there is a wide range of activities and adventure available locally in the district.'

True enough, there is — and that might include whitewater rafting, jet boating, canoeing, horse trekking, and even a bungy jump.

Above left: This pit-sawn cottage is used as a place to hold seminars.
Below: David and Sue, with Benji between them, relaxing near a pond in their grounds.

16 Richmond Station

Hosts: Oriel and Phil Vennell
Location: Rangitikei
Address: Richmond Station, Vennells'
Farmstay, 101 Mangapipi Road, Rewa,
RD10, Feilding
Phone: (06) 328-6780 or (025) 407-164 or
Free phone: 0800 220-172 PIN 1837
Fax: (06) 328-6780

Size: 484 hectares (1200 acres)
Stock: sheep, cattle
Accommodation: comfortable farmhouse,
three guest bedrooms: one queen-sized
room, one super king/twin room, one
twin room. Two private bathrooms
Nearest town: Hunterville 13 km

Out of Hunterville on the scenic route to Feilding I crossed via a short bridge the Rangitikei River. Soon, I was taking a side road that came to two white-painted gateposts dating to another era altogether. I had arrived at Richmond. Here in typical top-dressed hill country west of the Ruahine Ranges, Phil and Oriel Vennell have been running their farmstay business for over 20 years.

It all started, recalls Oriel, while they were on holiday in the Bay of Islands in 1979. A young Canadian tourist they met by chance admitted to them somewhat ruefully that he yet to engage in a good conversation with a local! Consequently they invited him to their property to rectify the situation.

In any event it was this incident that gave them the idea of inviting paying guests to stay at their home. These days many people do that.

Phil and Oriel also cater for what they refer to as 'lunch groups' — tourists on coach tours. Weather permitting, Oriel serves them their meal in their spacious garden, where pride of place belongs to two large walnut trees thought to be a century old.

It was a particularly lovely evening when Phil, tall and rangy, offered to take me around the property. Off we went with me sitting comfortably on the back of his farmbike. Presently we were sidling around a steep hillside where, on either side of the corrugated track, bleating ewes and wide-eyed lambs scattered every which way. The top of the hill provided a great view, not only of the farm complex below but also of the country side much further afield.

The Vennell connection with this land dates to 1898 when a 550-acre block was taken up by Elizabeth Vennell. Her husband, George, had died in 1876 and they had had six children. Her son, Frederick, would manage the property for her.

As a boy, Phil rode a horse the 14 km round trip to school at Rewa; his teacher, who boarded with Phil's parents, also rode to school.

In 1996, one of Phil and Oriel's four children, Justin, took over a 610-acre farm adjoining Richmond and today both properties are worked collectively and under the same name.

At the time of my visit, they were running 2200 Romney sheep and a mixed bag of cattle. The higher parts of the place ran up to 365 m and Phil often took people there not only to view the property but also to see the mountains of the Central North Island volcanic plateau.

Given his age, Phil is pretty much semi-retired these days, although that was not the impression I gained of him. But the fact that he's not as active as he was means that he can spend more time with guests and not be rushed, so a farm tour, for instance, can stretch to a relaxing couple of hours.

It's interesting to note that when Phil was a boy his father had two men working for him. Today, Justin works a much larger area of land on his own. Like his dad, Justin is tall and rangy; I reckoned he was coping well enough.

Phil's main hobby, he says, is trout fishing. They have a holiday home and a boat at Lake Taupo. However, he reckons that the local Rangitikei river has the lake beat hands down in that department. The fishermen they have had staying with them all enjoyed fishing the Rangitikei, Phil notes.

The Richmond homestead dates to 1973. The bedroom I slept in, complete with en suite, looks out over the front garden. At dawn, I strolled around the homestead's grounds. It would soon be time for me to move on. But it would, I mused, have been good to linger longer, to perhaps spend time at the river or take a longer tour of the farm than I had with

Phil. Yes, get up into their higher country and look towards the Ruahine Ranges, where I hunted professionally years ago. But they'd said I should come back anytime I wanted. Perhaps I would.

Left: The Richmond Station homestead and some of the garden.
Above: Milly the lamb and Butch the calf — both bottle-fed — get along famously.
Below: Late evening will soon close in at the station in the Rangitikei.

17 Mount Donald

Hosts: Jim and Lynne Sutherland
Location: Northern Wairarapa/Tararua
Address: Mount Donald, Newman, RD4,
Eketahuna 5480
Phone: (06) 375-8315
Fax: (06) 375-8391
E-mail: mountdonald@xtra.co.nz

Size: 484 hectares (1200 acres)
Stock: sheep, cattle
Accommodation: private guest wing
attached to homestead dating to 1900,
two bedrooms, one private bathroom,
one en suite
Nearest town: Eketahuna 5 km

It had been a wonderful lambing season, rangy Jim Sutherland was saying as, once again, I was being transported around a North Island property on the back of a versatile farmbike. The fact that plump Romney lambs were everywhere on his hill country farm only went to emphasise what he'd said. In fact, his flock of 2800 ewes had produced about 3600 little ones for farmer Jim and that wasn't harming his general disposition in the slightest.

Apart from his ewe flock, Jim had about 800 hoggets on the place and 120 Angus breeding cows so there were also many calves on display. Truly the spring is a lovely time to visit a farm like Mount Donald.

Soon, we had gained high ground: it was typical Wairarapa hill country, with, away to the west, the formidable barrier of the Tararua Ranges rising from the flat lands. Today stormclouds had gathered their troops about those high places and so they were mostly hidden from sight, but much closer a distinctive high point, Bruces Hill (710 m), could be clearly observed. The Mount Bruce farming district and the world-famous native bird reserve located here on State Highway 2, takes its name from the Bruce family who farmed here in the late 1880s and early 1890s.

The Sutherland connection with Mount Donald, says Jim, goes back to before the Second World War when his grandfather, also Jim, took over a block of leasehold land. He ran dairy cattle. Jim's father, Basil, and his uncle, Colin, began running the place in the early 1950s. They turned from dairy cattle to sheep and beef cattle. In 1970, Jim, not long

Left: The Mount Donald homestead.
Right: Jim Sutherland on the station with a storm brewing over the Tararua Ranges.
Below: Looking out from the homestead to stock-covered pastures.

out of his teens, became a partner in the farm. Later that decade they purchased a small, adjoining farm, making Mount Donald about 1500 acres (since reduced). In 1982 Jim and Lynne, who came from the King Country, were financially sound enough to buy out his uncle and, later, his father too.

The Sutherlands began their farmstays in 1992: 'We'd often meet tourists when we were taking sheep across the main road,' explains Lynne, 'and of course we'd hold up the traffic. But they never seemed to mind and many of them would take photographs. Quite often we'd end up talking to some of them and they'd be so interested in what we were doing we'd invite them to have a cup of tea at our place. Jim would often take them for a quick look about the farm. They all said they enjoyed it very much.'

And so did Jim and Lynne. They got a real charge out of meeting people from overseas and, not only talking about where they came from, but also explaining something about how they lived on a typical New Zealand farm. In any

event, they decided to do something about it.

To cater for their guests they developed a separate wing in their main, spacious homestead. It has a big, upstairs lounge that offers a grand view of their farm.

The farm has good walking and hiking tracks. It also has its own trout stream, where fishing is available all year round. Nearby at Eketahuna is a fine, 18-hole golf course while the Mount Bruce Wildlife Centre — a must to visit — is just 10 minutes' drive away.

I found Jim and Lynne fine company and their location is perfect for anyone from the capital city wanting a break in the country or for tourists travelling between Hawke's Bay and Wellington via the Wairarapa.

18 Waimoana Station

Hosts: Bill and Lynne Thompson
Location: Wairarapa
Address: Waimoana Station, Glenburn Road, RD3, Masterton
Phone: (06) 372-7732
Fax: (06) 372-7782
E-mail: waimoanastation@xtra.co.nz

Size: 1000 hectares (2471 acres)
Stock: sheep, cattle
Accommodation: three self-contained, three-bedroomed cottages located on various parts of the station
Nearest town: Masterton

I have now driven out to the splendid Wairarapa coastline — where Waimoana Station is located — on two separate occasions, once in the autumn and again, more recently, in the spring. It is about an hour's drive from Masterton.

Back in April 1996, I visited Glenburn Station that adjoins a part of Waimoana. (Glenburn would be one of the places I would include in the third of my Station Country books.) It was then that I met Bill and Lynne Thompson. They

had bought Waimoana in 1991 and, when I had coffee with them at their grand old homestead, they explained that they were doing farmstays on the place. Given their great location, and the fact they are a terrific couple, Waimoana was a logical choice to include in this book.

Both Bill and Lynne Thompson (the parents of five children) are from Canterbury, Bill having spent his life until 1991 on a farm on Banks Peninsula and Lynne coming from Christchurch itself.

Bill's family, he says, had farmed near Lake Ellesmere since about 1888 and so selling up and moving north represented a major step, but they have no regrets. In fact, as Lynne told me a few years ago, they loved it up here where the weather was so much kinder and, as Bill says with a farmer's pleased smile, 'The grass grows year-round.'

Waimoana Station was originally part of a 10,000-hectare block taken up by Hales and Murch in the 1850s. The block later came into the hands of the Cameron family in 1908. When Charlie Cameron died in 1943, the station passed on to his three sons and they split it up amongst themselves in 1956. The eldest son, Crawford, retained the fine homestead given to him and his bride as a wedding present in 1929, at the southern end of the station. He named his property Waimoana. And Waimoana remained in the Cameron family until the Thompsons arrived on the scene in 1991.

The Waimoana homestead, which is first glimpsed standing among exotic trees as you descend to the coast, is considered typical of the period. It is a huge, sprawling affair with extensive use of rimu panelling and ornate ceilings. Red deer trophies, dating from a period when the Wairarapa was a premier hunting ground, also add to a feeling that you have stepped into an entirely different era.

Left: The Waimoana homestead dates to 1920.
Below: A stand of karaka trees (with shiny leaves) fringing Waimoana's steep hilly terrain.

The homestead's two-acre grounds are a pleasure to stroll through. Free-ranging Peking ducks and strutting peacocks complement the overall scene and also make it seem far removed from Wellington, where many of their guests come from.

While much of the station is hilly, running up to 435 m, a good percentage of it is made up of attractive coastal flat lands, culminating in a 7-km boundary with Glenburn. On these sunny flats are eye-catching stands of karaka trees, while on the slopes stand cabbage trees. They are currently running 4000 Romney sheep and 250 head of Angus cattle.

There are three renovated cottages on Waimoana Station: The Scrubcutters' Hut, The Shepherd's House and the Beachcombers' Bach. They offer three individual styles of accommodation in which to relax in great surroundings. Dinner with Bill and Lynne at their 72-year-old homestead is by arrangement.

What to do on Waimoana? Well, the sea is nearby and that offers great fishing, diving, and snorkelling. According to Bill, this particular coastline is one of the truly untouched areas in the North Island. On the station itself are some pre-European sites. There is also a great walk along the coastline, passing through Glenburn, to Honeycomb Rock. The Department of Conservation (DOC) also controls a seal colony here.

Left: Peking ducks have the run of the homestead area.
Above: Bill Thompson looks out to sea.

19 Bowlands Station

Hosts: John and Philippa Falloon
Location: Bideford, Wairarapa
Address: Bowlands Station, Bideford, RD11, Masterton
Phone: (06) 372-4842
Fax: (06) 372-4855
E-mail: bowlands@xtra.co.nz

Size: 1737 hectares (4300 acres)
Stock: sheep, cattle, horses
Accommodation: three self-contained cottages, plus five bedrooms in an elegant, modern farm house
Nearest town: Masterton 22 km

I really couldn't think of a more lovely spot to wake up on a fine spring morning than in one of the three renovated farm cottages on Bowlands Station in the Wairarapa. This particular cottage, named 'The Woodshed', featured two bedrooms, a living room/kitchen, and a separate bathroom — all immaculately presented. The two other cottages that people can stay in are The Bakehouse and Hadleigh's.

The magnificent dwelling that the Falloons refer to as their 'house' mostly caters for business groups seeking a quiet country retreat where they can hold conferences. The Falloons have a number of suitable conference areas and facilities available and can accommodate 17 people at once.

In any event, I arose at The Woodshed. Presently, I strolled across the small lawn to look across a man-made lake to where John and Philippa Falloon live. Built in 1993 (to replace the old homestead that was destroyed by fire a year earlier), the Bowlands House looked wonderful with the early morning sunshine striking it. The lake was dug by John and his sons as a birthday gift for Philippa. It's safe to say that not everyone gets a lake for their birthday!

From my vantage point, I could also look across to an area named 'The Lawn' or 'The Park'. Many of the exotic trees that stood there dated to the 1860s, said Philippa. She told me that one of the trees, a Himalayan spruce, was considered the biggest such specimen in the Southern Hemisphere. Later, she also pointed out a splendid kahikatea reputed to be between 900 and 1000 years old.

On this particular morning, some of their South Suffolk sheep were grazing in the wooded area. The impression I gained might have leaped at me from the pages of a Thomas Hardy novel of a bygone rural England.

John Falloon, the charming ex-Minister of Agriculture, gave me a tour of some of the farms and surrounding countryside. Bowlands, says John, dates to 1842. At its peak it was about 15,000 acres and carried 6000 sheep. The station has been in his family since the 1880s.

What I found especially interesting were the many old buildings. The oldest, dating to the early 1860s, is the stables. It was built of kauri shipped down from Northland. Kauri (but mostly rimu) was also used in the construction of the four-bedroomed cottage known as The Bakehouse. The Woolshed, dating to 1902, was built of local matai and totara.

Bowlands was running 6000 Romney ewes, a mixed bunch of 460 cattle, and the 100 sheep that comprised their Suffolk stud. They also bred and trained thoroughbred horses for the polo circuit. Areas of the property had been planted with exotic trees as a long-term investment while new country was being developed for stock. John was hoping to run 12,000 stock units by mid-2000 with the help of manager Arthur Harrison.

Above left: The so-called 'Woodshed' is far from that.
Above: The Bowlands House.
Below: John and Philippa and their pet donkey outside the woolshed, which dates to 1902.

20 Papanui Station

Hosts: Bev and Cliff Inglis
Location: Ohariu Valley Road
Address: Mill Cottage Farmstays, Papanui Station, Boom Rock Road, Ohariu Valley, Wellington
Phone: (04) 478-8926

Size: 1300 hectares (3200 acres)
Stock: sheep, cattle
Accommodation: renovated farm cottage, two bedrooms, share bathroom with hosts
Nearest town: Wellington 17 km

On a windblasted headland, affording spectacular view of Cook Strait and a sun-hazed South Island, it seemed impossible that downtown Wellington was a mere 20 minutes' drive away. But that was the case here on Papanui Station located out of Johnsonville on the no-exit, winding Ohariu Valley Road.

While the farmstay business that Bev and Cliff Inglis run is located with the general homestead and woolshed complex of the station, it is operated separately to Papanui's other activities.

The Eastwick family own Papanui and have done so since 1926 when Captain John Eastwick, an Englishman from Kent and late of the Indian Army, purchased it from the Turnbull Estate. Papanui was then a thriving sheep station and the present woolshed and farmstay cottage,

then a single shepherd's accommodation, date to Turnbull's time.

There was still a lot of native timber, especially totara, on the place in 1926. John and his son, Richard, set about clearing and developing the rolling hill-country property of which 8 km is bounded by the sea.

By 1930 they were running 2500 Romney sheep and 50 cattle on Papanui's then 2000 acres. The yearly woolclip was 60 bales.

These days, according to Cliff, they carried 10,500 stock units at peak time (including lambs). The sheep were basically Romney cross-bred and the cattle were a South Devon/Angus cross.

I spotted a low-lying island located just off the coast. This unlikely place can be regarded as the birthplace of the Merino sheep industry in New Zealand. In 1834, a Scotsman, John

Bell Wright, took up residence on Mana Island. He brought 102 Merinos and a supply of hay with him from Port Jackson, across the Tasman. A year later he shipped a few bales of wool to Australia and this remains the first well-documented sale of New Zealand wool overseas.

Papanui's high country is truly wonderful, a sort of high plateau running up to Colonial Knob, which, at 460 m, is Wellington's highest point.

I saw many birds during my farm tour. Sometimes they spot a royal albatross along the coastline. In winter, seals venture here from Kaikoura. The fishing is great, says Cliff, particularly at Boom Rock.

The Papanui homestead area is at 90 m. Cliff and Bev's appealing cottage is situated on the banks of Mill Stream with steep hills rising behind it. From my comfortable bedroom I looked out at the woolshed.

Bev is a great cook and her main purpose during my visit seemed to be making sure I ate enough. Certainly you don't fade away staying on any farm or station around the country.

Both Cliff and Bev are into hiking and biking. They have been around most of New Zealand on cycling tours. Now that they are in their fifties their main ambition is to visit some of the places that their varied guests have come from.

**Left: Mill Cottage on Papanui Station is but 17 km from downtown Wellington.
Above: A lone cabbage tree stands in front of a section of the old woolshed. Mill Cottage is directly behind.
Below: Rain, sun, strong winds and mist. All that can happen within a very short time on Papanui Station, says Cliff Inglis.**

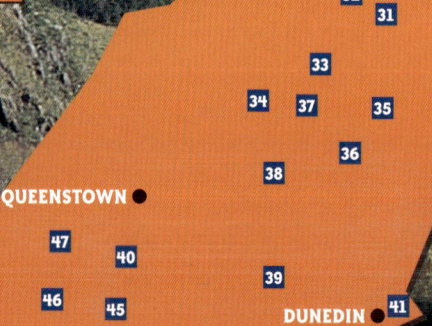

The South Island

Mataura Valley Station lies below the Eyre Mountains, p. 100.

21 Kairuru Station

Hosts: David and Wendy Henderson
Location: Takaka Hill, via Motueka
Address: Kairuru Station, State Highway 60, Takaka Hill, Motueka
Phone: (03) 528-8091 or (025) 337-457 or Free phone: 0800 524-787
Fax: (03) 528-8091
E-mail: kairuru@xtra.co.nz
Size: 1616 hectares (4000 acres)
Stock: Corriedale/Perendale cross-bred sheep, Hereford and Hereford/Shorthorn cross-bred cattle
Accommodation: The Homestead — two bedrooms, one double room and one twin room, one private bathroom. Two self-contained cottages: Kea Cottage — two bedrooms, one double room and one twin room, plus attic; Pipit Cottage — two bedrooms, one queen-sized room and one twin room
Nearest town: Motueka 17 km

I t was late evening and the end of a magical day: I'd spent the last three days walking the Abel Tasman Track and now I was relaxing with a cup of tea in hand on the verandah of a farm cottage with a commanding, panoramic view spread out before me. I had a bird's eye vista of the sweeping beach and estuary at Marahau, where the Abel Track can either start or end.

Presently, I heard a dog bark in the distance; then a man's voice carried to me. Curious, I hopped over a fence, disturbed some cattle and sheep, and then spotted, way below, a tiny, ant-like figure and some equally small sheep being mustered across a steep hillface. That had to be David Henderson, whom I'd yet to meet. He'd spent all of his life on Kairuru Station. I wondered how many times he'd mustered this hill country.

The station was taken up by David's grandfather in 1910. Previously owned by a man named Smith, almost all of it was in heavy forest. Extensive tree-felling continued on the place during David's father's time and even today some 700 acres bordering Abel Tasman National Park are still forest-clad. Out there are potentially troublesome feral goats, wild pigs and red deer. Many of these wild animals drift back and forth between the station and the national park because Kairuru's boundary here is unfenced.

These days, David runs 2500 sheep and 140 head of cattle. The ewes were lambing while I was there — the real bonus of taking a farmstay vacation in the spring. Dusk was falling now at Pipit Cottage. From the kitchen/living room area I could see sheep and cattle spread over the station's steep hills. Also, the birds, soon to turn in for the night, were going at near full blast: tui, bellbirds, a pretty fantail hovered outside the kitchen window; the eye-catching wattle trees, gloriously yellow only a short time ago, had lost almost all of their colour.

Then I heard a sound — 'kea ... keeea ... keeea!' — I expect I'll always associate with the Milford Tack. I darted back to the verandah. Yes, it was a kea. I already knew it was about 550 m here — this seemed to me to be well out of the usual range of New Zealand's number-one personality bird. Or was it? The other cottage was called 'Kea', after all, wasn't it?

Later, I headed on up to the homestead for dinner. I'd dressed for the part in my RM Williams shirt and moleskins; better make the right impression.

The homestead had been built, Wendy informed me, 20 years ago. They had built it on the site of the original homestead, which had burned down. They had utilised timber from the station with which to build it: Douglas fir and totara. The end result has a lovely, warm feel about it.

Wendy, Canterbury-born, explained that most of their visitors had a good look about the place with the slim, affable David. There was also a special paddock where they kept pet sheep, pigs, and goats, and that always proved popular. Also, there was a historic marble quarry on the place and many found that fascinating to wander around.

Local attractions include of course the Abel Tasman National Park, an absolute wonderland in my opinion. Wendy often suggests that

Left: The Kairuru homestead.
Above: Pipit Cottage.
Below: Corriedale sheep grazing near Pipit Cottage. The beach at Marahau can be seen in the background.

their visitors take a day trip on the track. That could include a launch trip from Kaiteriteri to Totaranui (the park headquarters) and back, or a combination walk/launch trip. The options available to park visitors are as many as they are varied. Also close to hand is Golden Bay. To get there you drive over Takaka Hill, which, on the descent into Golden Bay, offers a staggering view of the north-west Nelson National Park. The whole Nelson area, with its wonderful climate, where you can spend one day on the coast and another in the mountains, is hard to beat.

22 Netherwood Station

Hosts: Bruce and Nola Dick
Location: Waihopai River valley
Address: Netherwood, RD6,
Blenheim 7321
Phone: (03) 572-4044
Fax: (03) 572-4043
E-mail: nbdick@xtra.co.nz
Size: 1212 hectares (3000 acres)

Stock: Merino sheep, Hereford/Angus cross-bred cattle
Accommodation: Two bedrooms annexed to main homestead, one queen bed and two single beds. Private bathroom. One booking per night. Meals available. Also tidy self-contained cottage
Nearest town: Blenheim 50 km

'Put your gear in there and I'll go swing the billy.' They were almost the first words that Bruce Dick had spoken to me. I had to smile; I might have just turned up at a mustering camp in the hills rather than at first-rate farmstay accommodation way up the valley of the Waihopai River.

I dumped some of my gear where I would spend the night — a lovely bedroom with a delightful view of the garden — and then went and joined Bruce and his wife, Nola, for a welcome cup of tea.

Earlier, I'd left Highway 63 not far from Renwick and had then taken a dead-end 50 km road that probes deep into the mountains. There was light snow on the distant tops, gum trees and wattle trees in yellow flower lined the road

and in green paddocks, lambs were leaping about or lying quietly with their mothers.

As the miles passed and the surrounding country became more stunning, I was aware of the historic significance of this particular valley. In April 1850, early runholders Dashwood and Mitchell and a whaler named Harris crossed it and were credited with being the first Europeans to make a successful overland crossing between Nelson and Canterbury.

Soon, the Netherwood homestead, situated on a bench above the river, came into sight. After the turn-off to the homestead there is another 10 km of roadway. Further on there are another four stations that, like Netherwood Station, all produce super-fine Merino wool.

In any event, I was soon having that cup of tea with Bruce and Nola in their home. They both come from Otago, Bruce a farmer from Hindon and Nola hailing from the Catlins. They moved up here seven years ago and, as they had done at their small Hindon farm, carried on with their farmstay business.

Bruce, I'd noticed, had a rather satisfied look about him. Fair enough. They had just finished shearing their 3000 sheep. Lending a hand had been their son Glenn, 23, who was home on holiday. Mostly Bruce and his wife do all the work on the place themselves. No easy thing but that's the way it is today for many a high-country family.

Netherwood came into being at the time the giant-sized Hillersden run was split up following the First World War. The homestead built after that still stands. Today, it is used for anyone wanting an inexpensive farm holiday. People staying there, says Nola, can look after themselves or take some of their meals at the main homestead.

Nola, a tramper who has walked the major South Island tracks, tells me there are fine walks to be had on the farm. There is also a terrific swimming hole a short walk from the homestead. Bruce takes people out on the farm, up to high ridges where the view is spectacular. There are wild deer and pigs on the place; the pigs often prove troublesome at lambing time.

Local attractions include the now famous Marlborough wine trail. Indeed, the Grove Mill vineyards and winery are located at the foot of the valley.

Left: The Netherwood homestead.
Above: The Waihopai River forms a deep pool below Netherwood.
Below: Guests can also stay in the old homestead.

23 Tophouse

Hosts: Melody and Mike Nicholls
Location: Saint Arnaud, Nelson Lakes
Address: Tophouse, RD2, Nelson
Phone: (03) 521-1848 or
Free phone: 0800 867-468
Fax: (03) 521-1848
E-mail: tophouse@clear.net.nz

Size: 300 hectares (700 acres)
Stock: Angus cattle, assorted pets
Accommodation: historic hotel, four guest bedrooms, share facilities. Also four two-bedroomed, self-contained cottages
Nearest town: Saint Arnaud 9 km

On a particularly fine September afternoon, Melody Nicholls was flat out at Tophouse, the old hotel, and now a farmstay, that she and her husband, Mike, purchased in 1988. She was simultaneously showing some visitors around the hotel's interesting features while supervising afternoon tea for a party of four.

When the Nicholls arrived on the scene, the hotel was badly run down; it was considered too far gone to be restored to its former glory. But a great deal has changed at Tophouse since then. Rather a lot went on there before then, too.

The Tophouse story starts in 1842 when a 23-year-old surveyor, John Cotterel, acting on behalf of the New Zealand Company, set off from Nelson with a view to finding a practicable overland route to Blenheim. Cotterel travelled with a friend and an indispensable Maori guide, reaching the Clarence River, a distance of over 300 km, in two weeks. On their return journey their Maori guide took them to see the jewel of the Nelson Lakes National Park, Lake Rotoiti. Cotterel would be credited with being the first European to gaze upon its lovely waters and stunning mountains.

The route he opened up soon became the major stock route linking Nelson and Blenheim and beyond. At Tophouse, roughly midway between both points, a hotel would be built and it became the main stopover point on the journey. For around 130 years, before its liquor licence was cancelled in 1969, Tophouse was a welcome sight for drovers and wagoners and, later, motorists.

Left: Tophouse.
Right: The Nicholls boys: Karl holding
Hoki-Poki the lamb and Jared nursing
Quackery the duck.
Below: Mallards at Lake Rotoiti.

When Melody and Mike Nicholls took on a near-derelict Tophouse, it was with a view to restoring a vital link with New Zealand's early history. Living on the premises, they spent six months working on the place before it was ready to take guests. What they did not expect was just how popular Tophouse would become.

Melody and Mike entertain as many as 16,000 casual visitors in a year. They are open, free of charge, to people who are passing by and simply want to see the old hotel. They serve refreshments from 9 a.m. to 5 p.m. and sell souvenirs and crafts.

Because overnight stays at the hotel proved so popular they built four two-bedroomed, self-contained cottages nearby. They are often used by family groups wanting self-contained accommodation and by skiers using the Rainbow Skifield in the Saint Arnaud Range.

On the farm itself, Mike runs a herd of Angus cattle, sourced from Molesworth Station, the largest cattle property in the country. Angus are hardy and they need to be as the Tophouse country starts at 760 m and runs up to 1300 m. Its winters are long and hard. A nine-hole golf-course has also recently been opened on the property.

Apart from the Rainbow Skifield, the main attraction is Lake Rotoiti. The DOC information office at Saint Arnaud is the place to check out what the lake has to offer.

One thing I especially enjoyed about my visit to Tophouse was the atmosphere; past and present are very much alive here.

24 Kahutara Homestead

Hosts: John and Nikki Smith
Location: Kaikoura
Address: Kahutara Homestead, Dairy Farm Road, Kaikoura
Phone: (03) 319-5580
Fax: (03) 319-5580
E-mail: kahutarahomestead@xtra.co.nz

Size: 808 hectares (2000 acres)
Stock: sheep, cattle
Accommodation: excellent homestead featuring three bedrooms, one queen-sized room, one twin room and one single, one luxury en suite
Nearest town: Kaikoura 20 km

The woolshed on Kahutara was built, says John Smith, some time after Greenhills Station was subdivided in about 1910: its red-painted sides had faded to clearly reveal the old weatherboards beneath, and, while corrugated iron was used as a building material right from the early days of settlement, this particular iron roofing, glinting in the early evening sun, was comparatively new.

There's something about old woolsheds that really appeals to me. While this particular woolshed was nothing out of the ordinary, the same old story applied. Maybe it's the so familiar smell inside them, the way grease from wool and endless streams of urine have impregnated the wooden floorboards. Or perhaps it's because images of shearers and rouseabouts fill my mind. Certainly this old

woolshed would have a good story to tell.

The Kahutara run (43,738 acres at its peak) was taken up by Robert Fyffe in the 1840s. The Bullen brothers took it on in 1866. They ran it in conjunction with Greenhills Station. The brothers shipped in cattle and horses from Newcastle, in New South Wales. Over 70,000 sheep ranged on their land in the early 1890s. Subdivision began in 1896.

John Smith, an amiable type, comes from the Kaikoura district; his father, Jack, had a 4000-acre property in the northern Kaikouras. John spent his early working days mustering locally, later, he did the same thing on Walter Peak Station, near Queenstown. Later still, he cashed in when lucrative markets for venison opened up in Germany and the United States.

It was in 1974 that John and Nikki Smith,

married four years, purchased Kahutara. The station took its name from the river itself, which you cross en route to the station. The Smiths run 2800 Corriedale sheep and some 250 cattle — the usual Black Angus/Hereford cross that do so well in the high country. Indeed, the station runs up to 490 m and John often takes people up there to take in what he describes as a magnificent view. He also likes to take people over the 1880s horse mail route.

Nikki Smith is also a local, hailing from a farm up the Blue Duck Valley, just 22 km north-east of Kaikoura. One of six children, Nikki was into horses from an early age. After her pony-club days, she competed at shows in various equestrian events. The Smiths' three daughters were just as keen on horses as their parents were. In the dining room of the Kahutara homestead (dating to the same general period as the woolshed) there are coloured ribbons and pennants on the wall to show the girls' success in the saddle. At the time of my visit, the Smiths had three brood mares, which were all away at stud.

The location, says Nikki, is ideal for anyone who wants not only to spend time in the country but also to take advantage of Kaikoura's now world-famous attractions: the year-round Whale Watch, swimming with dolphins, deep-sea fishing and bird-watching excursions.

Left: Parts of the Kahutara homestead date to around 1910.
Top: The Kaikoura Range dominates the background, while the Kahutara River runs to the right and the road leading to the station is to the left of this view.
Above: John and Nikki; Rose is John's favourite working dog.

25 Pahau Pastures

Host: Di Bethell
Location: North Canterbury
Address: Pahau Pastures, St Leonards Road, Culverden, North Canterbury
Phone: (03) 315-8023 or (025) 362-530
Fax: (03) 315-8966
E-mail: pahau.pastures@xtra.co.nz

Size: 1416 hectares (3500 acres)
Stock: sheep, cattle
Accommodation: historic homestead, three bedrooms, one en suite, one private bathroom
Nearest town: Culverden 4.5 km

The sun wasn't shining and it was the wrong season to see the spectacular display of daffodils that run riot in the spring as I drove down the driveway towards the grand old homestead at Pahau Pastures.

This was a rather 'soft' afternoon in autumn with drizzle falling and the hill country at the back of the station hiding in the mist. No matter. Such weather had a certain charm all of its own.

As I arrived, Di Bethell was busy making pumpkin soup in her sprawling farmhouse-style kitchen. She had three guests for the weekend. They were all from Christchurch (100 km away). In fact, they were duck hunters and this was the start of the duck hunting season. Right now they were out at a pond on the station and wouldn't be back until later. Di said they'd been coming here for years.

It was in 1852 that two Englishmen, George Duppa and Henry Young, took up a 122,000-hectare block of land here in North Canterbury. They would split it between them into roughly equal parts. Young named his intended station Culverden, after a property he had owned in the South of England. Duppa's land, more to the east, was named St Leonards.

In 1877 St Leonards Station was subdivided.

Richard Bethell purchased what became Pahau Pastures. Also from England, Bethell already owned land south of Christchurch, which he had named Burnham, after his birthplace, Burnham Beeches, in Surrey. As Di explained, that is how today's Burnham (where the military camp is located) was named.

Pahau Pastures has been in the same family for five generations. The original house was built in 1880 as a manager's residence. It was made of kauri, the timber having been shipped down from Northland. When Marmaduke (Richard Bethell's only son) and his wife, Thyra, came to live here they decided to enlarge it and employed Christchurch architect Samuel Hurst-Seager. Working to his design, four bedrooms were added, a smoking room, office, drawing room, and quarters for the servants, who had their own sitting room. Encasing all this was a splendid verandah, positioned for winter sun.

It was Marmaduke and Thrya, says Di, who were responsible for planting the English-style woodland garden that dates to the period when they enlarged the homestead (1904). The woodland setting provides an essential shelter belt but does not restrict the amount of sun or obscure their view across the Amuri Plains.

By the time it was David and Di's turn to move into the homestead, a long period of general neglect called for urgent restoration, alterations and some modernising. This would prove to be a compatible blend of old and new, a credit to David (who died in 1998) and Di's input, and that of their architect, Nick Courtney, and local builder, Robert Honeybone.

These days Hugh Bethell, Di's oldest son, looks after the day-to-day running of the property with two others, while a younger son, Sam, farms nearby. At the time of my visit, they were carrying 6500 Corriedale ewes, 25 South Suffolk rams, 25 Corriedale rams and 1000 Hereford/Angus cattle. A big operation. A tour of the station is considered a must.

Local attractions, says Di, include any number of outdoor activities including skiing, jet-boating, golf, horse riding, and tramping. The hot thermal pools at Hanmer Springs are only 37 km away.

Above left: The homestead at Pahau Pastures.
Left: Several interesting old buildings remain at the station. This was the single shepherds' accommodation.
Above: Peking ducks seen a short walk from the homestead.
Below: South Suffolk sheep look very well in this North Canterbury setting.

26 Whispering Pines

Hosts: Jean and Russell Adams
Location: Inchbonnie, Westland
Address: Whispering Pines, Inchbonnie, RD1, Kumara 7871, Westland
Phone: (03) 738-0153
Fax: (03) 738-0353
Size: 540 hectares (1334 acres)
Stock: cross-bred sheep, cross-bred cattle, red deer

Accommodation: refurbished 1930s sawmiller's cottage, two bedrooms, one double bed, four single beds. Also accommodation at main homestead — two bedrooms, double bed or twin, share bathroom. Plus campervan facilities

Nearest town: Kumara 30 km

An interesting aspect of staying at farmstays around the country is the various types of accommodation they may provide. Here at Whispering Pines, it mostly came down to a lovely old sawmiller's cottage dating to the 1930s, a period when sawmilling

was the prime industry of Westland. With two bedrooms, an open fire, bath and shower but no television or telephone it offers an ideal escape from the pressures of normal day-to-day living. Which is why, during the September school holidays, a Christchurch family were staying there. The children were keen to tell me they had seen a tame weka (which resided near the cottage) with four brand-new chicks.

At any rate, I found myself staying with Russell and Jean in the homestead. It was designed along traditional English lines by the English-born wife of Randall Topliss, the first owner of the farm after it was subdivided off the old Bruce Estate about 1916.

In 1868 a Scot, Thomas Bruce, looked for land in Westland. He found it here in the valley of the Orangipuku River, which drains into the south side of Lake Brunner (the biggest lake on the West Coast). Here he took up 2697 acres.

By 1900 Bruce had increased his land holdings to 6000 acres. Officially it was known as the Bruce Estate. Locals, however, referred to it as 'Bruce's Paddock'. Also Bruce had a summer range block for his 13,000 Merinos near Otira. Subdivision of the Bruce Estate began in 1916 and Whispering Pines is thought to have been one of the first blocks to be sold.

Canterbury-born Alfred Adams bought the farm in 1954. His son, Russell took over in 1968. Today, he runs 600 cross-bred sheep, 150 cross-bred cattle, and 200 red deer. Much of his farm is still covered in native forest.

At Whispering Pines they are flexible when it comes down to the individual needs of their guests. While the cottage is self-contained, if they prefer, guests can have breakfast at the homestead. Jean will also provide what they might need for a breakfast or dinner and they can cook it at the cottage. There are also several good restaurants in the area.

The cottage at Whispering Pines had a lot going for it. An English couple certainly thought that as, having stayed there for two weeks, they returned a year or so later for two months; Jean says they are coming back again in 2001.

What this valley has to offer is in harmony with a break from city life. There are fine bush walks to enjoy, birds to observe; I saw so many pukeko and weka on the farm that I kidded Russell he must be farming them, too.

Then there is Lake Brunner, located within walking distance of the cottage. This is a great spot for swimming and boating, and it also offers fine trout fishing. However, Russell, a keen fisherman, much prefers to fish at the small Lake Poerua, not far away. He also points out that the Taramakau River is great for salmon.

Russell is only too pleased to show people around the farm. Like any farm, there's always something going on. Often he shears a sheep, to show people how it's done and Jean then demonstrates how she spins the wool and, from it, makes handknitted sweaters, hats, blankets and other assorted items. Woollen goods made by Jean have ended up in many parts of the world.

Above left: The homestead at Whispering Pines. The Hohonu Range rises in the background.
Below left: Adams Cottage — a sawmiller's dwelling dating from the 1930s.
Below: Cross-bred sheep graze on the green pastures of Whispering Pines.

27 The Homestead

Hosts: Kevin and Noeleen Williams
Location: Fox Glacier
Address: The Homestead, Cook Flat Road, PO Box 25, Fox Glacier
Phone: (03) 751-0835
Fax: (03) 751-0835

Size: 1132 hectares (2800 acres)
Stock: sheep, dairy cattle
Accommodation: fine homestead with three guest bedrooms, two queen-sized beds, two single beds; two en suites
Nearest town: Fox Glacier 0.5 km

There was fresh snow on Mount Cook, the late afternoon sun sparkled on whatever it touched, and the tourist village of Fox Glacier was looking a treat.

Along this narrow shelf of land contained between mountain and sea is Kevin and Noeleen Williams' station, The Homestead. It is the biggest property here, but then, Kevin's family have always had the monopoly on real estate around Fox Glacier. It began in the early 1890s when Kevin's grandfather, Fred, came from Gillespies Beach and took up 25,000 acres.

Typically, most of Fred's run is heavily clad with forest, the most dominant tree being the mighty totara. Totara lives to around 800 years and is a most durable timber. The Maori used it to build their great canoes. The Europeans found it ideal for many purposes; house frames and piles, railway sleepers, telegraph poles and for fenceposts. Many of the old, moss-clad fencelines and huts you see around Fox Glacier today were made of totara milled in the late 1890s and early-to-mid-1900s.

Originally, Fred ran a herd of dairy cattle, supplying the gold-mining community at nearby Gillespies Beach with milk and other dairy products. Later, he ran beef cattle — Herefords exclusively. The Hereford is still the most common breed of cattle on the West Coast.

Today, Kevin Williams runs 1500 Perendale sheep and 900 head of cattle, predominantly Herefords. Perendales, he says, are well-suited to wet conditions and they are largely able to fend for themselves. At the time of my visit the cows were calving and they made a wonderful sight on the morning of my stay as they soaked up the sun on the flat lands that give way to 'a land uplifted high'. This is where Kevin, nearing retirement age now, has lived all of his life.

Nowadays, Kevin works the place with his son, Paul. They take on extra help when needed. They mostly use farmbikes for stock work but even so, the horse is still the most useful way of getting around the country when mustering cattle, especially if that means they have to ford the snow-fed Cook and Fox Rivers.

The sun was still shining in the late evening as, following a photographic foray to Fox Glacier village, I returned to my night's accommodation at The Homestead. As I drove along the unsealed driveway leading to the homestead, I observed a spur-winged plover nestling in lush green grass and closer to the homestead a paradise duck was perched on a totara fencepost. I also saw five pukeko lurking hopefully around the back door — it's no wonder the birdlife is such a hit with the guests.

The homestead, dating to the mid-1890s, features many of its original lead-light windows. My bedroom for the night, complete with en suite, had a lovely view of the mountains rising above the nearby village.

It was Noeleen, from Christchurch originally but very much a 'West Coaster' now, who explained to me that they had been doing farmstays for over 30 years. It had started because accommodation had been difficult to find between Franz Josef and Haast — a situation that remains true today.

The busy season runs from early November through to late May. Having said that, every season on the West Coast has its own special charm and winter weather can be surprisingly good.

While Kevin often takes people on a tour of the place, they find most people stay with them because of their close proximity to two of New Zealand's outstanding tourist attractions: Fox Glacier itself and Lake Matheson, known for its mirror-like reflections of Mount Cook and Mount Tasman. Also popular is Gillespies Beach with its resident seal colony where as many as 1500 seals may gather during the winter.

Above left: The Homestead at Fox Glacier is within walking distance of the village.
Left: Kevin, Noeleen, and Chancey the corgi. The prominent peak is La Perouse (3079 m).
Below: Fox Glacier itself with the sun just about gone for the day.

28 Mulvaney Farmstay

Hosts: Malai and Peter Millar
Location: Bruce Bay, South Westland
Address: Mulvaney Farmstay, Condon Road, Bruce Bay, South Westland
Phone: (03) 751-0865
Fax: (03) 751-0865
E-mail: mulvaney@xtra.co.nz
Size: 700 hectares (1729 acres)

Stock: cattle
Accommodation: renovated 1920s farmhouse; two guest bedrooms in farmhouse, one double, one twin; also detached accommodation, double en suite
Nearest town: Haast/Fox Glacier approximately 55 km either way

North of Haast, but about three-quarters of an hour's drive on to Fox Glacier, there is a signpost on the side of State Highway 6, which indicates that your destination — Mulvaney Farmstay — is down Condon Road. The Bannock Brae Range looms progressively taller as you take this unsealed route. Presently you reach a farmhouse dating to the 1920s.

This farmhouse, this land, has been home for Malai and Peter Millar since 1980. The property, however, has been in his family since 1865.

John Mulvaney, Peter's great-grandfather, came to the West Coast with a friend in search of gold. They worked the wild, windswept beaches where the big rivers rampaged down from brooding mountains. They headed south and eventually came to the Mahitahi River. It

would appear that they had found very little of the precious yellow metal because John's friend left him here. John, however, liked what he saw: a big, heavily forested land sweeping back to mountains unlike any he had known.

John took out a pastoral lease for 5000 acres. Running from the coast to the mountain tops, its boundaries were the Jacobs River to the north and the Mahitahi River to the south. It was the usual story for the Irishman: he cleared land, built a home and ran cattle. He named his run Bannock Brae, a name that is still used today.

It seems that likely women were even more difficult to locate on the West Coast than gold because John Mulvaney would live on his own for 20 years until he advertised in Ireland for a wife-to-be. He was successful and the result of what turned out to be a happy union was nine children.

In 1980, Peter Millar was living in Australia. He was married to Malai, whom he'd met in Thailand. Peter often thought about home; the West Coast, he knew, was in his blood. When the opportunity came to take on the family farm, he seized the opportunity. No matter that it was run down, and that prospects for farming weren't encouraging, he wanted it. But today he can still smile ruefully about the kind of home he brought his city-born wife to. What

Above left: The Millar's farmhouse.
Above: The Mahitahi River near Peter and Malai's farmstay.

Malai found here was a house with no electricity, no running water, no inside toilet and no telephone. As Peter often said in those early days: things could only get better. Which, of course, they did. Today, Malai loves her life on the West Coast.

Peter runs 150 Hereford/Limousin cattle. He has done well in local beef competitions, taking out first place several times. In 1994, he took out fourth place in the National Competition. Carlin, the Millars' 16-year-old son, also worked on the place. He was keen on horses — a 'West Coaster' who wanted to be nowhere else.

Farm tours? Malai takes people out with her on a farmbike. It is no problem, she says, because the farm is well-roaded. She often goes walking with people too. Malai is also the one responsible for serving delicious Thai meals. Malai likes to show any interested guests how to prepare such a meal.

Local attractions include Fox Glacier and Haast. Some of the Millars' guests had been on a jetboat ride on the Waiatoto River and found that a thrilling experience.

29 Glenview

Hosts: Andrew and Karen Hart
Location: Methven, Canterbury Plains
Address: Glenview, 142 Hart Road, State Highway 72, Methven, RD12 Rakaia
Phone: (03) 302-8620 or (025) 335-136
Fax: (03) 302-8650
E-mail: ahart@voyager.co.nz
Size: 480 hectares (1200 acres)

Stock: Coopworth/Romney cross-bred sheep, Simmental cross-bred cattle
Accommodation: modern farmhouse, three bedrooms, one private bathroom, plus a detached double unit close to the farmhouse
Nearest town: Methven 10 km

Andrew Hart was working with his dogs when I caught up with him one brisk autumn morning. They were shifting some of his 2600 ewes at the time, the dogs making it look easy.

Although they had had guests staying the previous night, it was really that time of the year when the summer tourist season was over and the winter one had yet to start.

Almost certainly Glenview was once a part of a much bigger property, at a time when big stations sprawled over the Canterbury Plains. It was part of the Spaxton Station that ran from

Methven to the edge of the mountains. Andrew McFarlane Hart took the place on in 1923 and that it has remained in the family ever since.

Glenview is located one hour's drive from Christchurch on the Inland Scenic Route of Highway 72. There is only one farm between it and the Mount Hutt Range. From most parts of Glenview there is what Andrew calls their 'million-dollar view' of the Mount Hutt Skifield. The country's most reliable snow seems only just beyond the farm's north-western boundary fence, such is the clarity of the air at 450 m.

The Harts and their two teenage children, Jonathan and Renee, love meeting new people. As Andrew says, 'Our philosophy has always been relaxed and informal. We're not a "dude" ranch, we're a working family. People are more than welcome to come along and participate in whatever it is we happen to be doing that day.'

Andrew fondly remembers one lovely summer's day when he was showing some North Americans around the farm. They were fascinated by some cows and their recently born calves. Andrew suggested that they sit down and keep still. They all did just that. Presently, the cows' curiosity became too much and they came over for a closer look and even sniffed the strangers in their midst. They all thought that was wonderful, says Andrew.

In terms of the meals provided, the accent here at Glenview is one of good traditional 'Kiwi' fare served with complementary wine.

Given its splendid location in the shadow of the mountains, Glenview is on the doorstep for outdoor pursuits. Jetboating in the Rakaia Gorge is always popular, so is bushwalking,

ballooning, parachuting, salmon and trout fishing, skiing, and horse riding. All of these activities can be enjoyed within a short drive of Glenview.

There are also some good restaurants in Methven. During the ski season, the town really buzzes and becomes the Canterbury Plains' version of Queenstown, minus the glitz.

Left: The Glenview farmhouse.
Below: Some of Glenview's sheep line up reluctantly for a photograph; Andrew is to the left.
Bottom: The detached unit for people to stay in.

30 Kawatea Farmstay

Hosts: Kerry and Judy Thacker
Location: Okains Bay, Banks Peninsula
Address: Kawatea Farmstay, Okains Bay,
Banks Peninsula
Phone: (03) 304-8621
Fax: (03) 304-8621
Size: 566 hectares (1400 acres)

Stock: Angus cross-bred cattle, Perendale
sheep
Accommodation: historic homestead
dating to 1901, three bedrooms, one en
suite, one guest bathroom
Nearest town: Akaroa 20 km

To my way of thinking there can be few lovelier places in the country than Banks Peninsula. Fortunate indeed is the large Thacker family that has lived here ever since John Edward Thacker, a coastal trader, stepped ashore at Okains Bay and bought a small section of land where he built a cottage. An Irishman, Thacker increased his land holdings until he finally owned 10,000 acres, which he named Highlands. All but a small portion of this land is still retained by the family. Later on, when the land was subdivided, coastal 'Kawatea' came into being.

With his high school days behind him, and not yet 17, Kerry Thacker took over the running of the farm from his father in 1962. Now, he and

his son, Adam, 23, work the place together.

I doubt if I have ever seen a more appealing spot than Kawatea, with its lovely green hills sweeping down to the coastal cliffs. In this setting, Kerry Thacker has spent most of his life. Here he has enjoyed fishing, diving, and sailing.

When I arrived at Kawatea, Judy Thacker explained that the menfolk were out in their hill country working on a new fenceline. Did I want to catch up with them out there?

So off we soon set in my Trooper, with Judy chattering away in answer to my questions. They had gone into farmstays in 1988. It was something they had talked about doing for quite some time.

'We hadn't travelled,' says Judy, 'and so

the basic idea was to bring people from other countries to us. That way we could learn about where they came from and what their lifestyles were like.'

By following a rough track along the indented coastline, we came to Little Okains Bay. The story goes that long ago, a Maori, leaping from his canoe and reaching the beach, looked about him: he saw the heavily forested hills above him; he knew that the coast and the sea here were bountiful, and that the climate was most agreeable. 'Kawatea!' he declared. Kerry says this means: 'This is the place I can make my home!' It can mean a state of mind, or a certain feel one has for a place.

Many Maori artefacts have been found on the coast, where there was a pa on a prominent headland. They are now mostly housed in the Maori and Colonial Museum in Okains Bay.

Once European settlement of Banks Peninsula began, the abundant forests were cut down, and Okains Bay was no exception to that rule. Many of those trees were the mighty totara — hard and durable wood much used for fencing in the early days. Here on Kawatea many old totara fenceposts still stand as they have for over 120 years.

With Okains Bay behind us, we came to higher ground. Angus cattle grazed in pale sunshine. Looking across Pegasus Bay I could see the sun-hazed Kaikoura Range and more to the north-west arose the main Southern Alps.

The cattle, I would later be told, were predominantly Angus crossed with Friesians and Herefords. They run about 500 of them. Kawatea also runs around 500 ewes — Perendales, which make easy work of the steepest country on the place.

Both Judy and Adam love their sheep. In the spring they might hand-feed as many as 20 lambs and so visitors have the opportunity to help out. One of the lambs they raised is now eight years old. He is a Merino called Chewey (because he ate so much as a young fellow).

When he was a lamb, Chewey was often in the homestead. These days, he lives with other tame sheep in a paddock next to the homestead, where they enjoy being fed stale bread.

Later, we caught up with Kerry and Adam. They were glad to take a break. Presently, Judy and I went on our way. She says that an ideal length of visit here is two nights and three days. This allows people to explore the farm, where there are many lovely beaches to poke about. Shellfish abound and there is even a seal colony to observe. Nearby Akaroa is also an interesting place to visit.

And of course you stay in a grand old homestead, which has 12 rooms, most of them featuring native timbers and stained-glass windows.

Left: Among a stand of exotic trees is the imposing Kawatea homestead.
Below: On a headland on Kawatea, above Okains Bay, are a few Angus cattle. The Southern Alps can be seen in the background.

31 Holbrook Station

Hosts: Alister and Lesley France
Location: Mackenzie Country
Address: Holbrook Station,
State Highway 8, between Burkes Pass
and Lake Tekapo, PO Box 4, Fairlie
Phone: (03) 685-8535 or (025) 387-974
Fax: (03) 685-8534
E-mail: lesley@holbrook.co.nz

Size: 14,000 hectares (35,000 acres)
Stock: Merino sheep, Hereford/Angus
cattle
Accommodation: comfortable self-
contained cottage, separate from main
farmhouse, three bedrooms
Nearest town: Lake Tekapo, 12 km

The brittle leaves of autumn, the muted reds and golds of poplar trees, were falling like raindrops about the old sheep yards at the Glenrock Station homestead complex. Here, Alister and Donald France were working with around 2000 of their sheep. Lending an enthusiastic hand were Brute, a big huntaway, and Ralph, a spunky Jack Russell. Ralph likes to think he's a sheepdog, too.

This same scene has been taking place here on the Mackenzie Country from only a short time after the legendary sheep stealer, James Mackenzie, went by this way en route with his stolen Merinos to Otago and into Southland.

There are three separate blocks involved in the Holbrook farmstay set-up: Holbrook itself was once a part of Sawdon Station, first taken up in 1858. In the early days it was commonplace to see a dozen bullock teams camped around the Sawdon homestead. The Holbrook subdivision dates to 1912.

In 1917, Glenrock, the main centre of farming operations, was taken off Rollesby Station (established in 1857). In 1960, David France (Alister and Donald's father) purchased Glenrock. The family added Holbrook to that property in 1979 and the Rollesby Range lease in 1989. Collectively, this adds up to 14,000

Above: Lesley takes a coffee break outside their farm cottage.
Right: With autumn leaves falling, Alister and Donald are busy at the Glenrock sheep yards.

hectares — on which they run 10,000 sheep and 400 cross-bred cattle. They also grow oats for winter feed and a cash crop.

While such numbers of sheep are common on big stations in the South Island, they can be daunting for a farmer with a small-holding in Europe. Two Swiss farmers who stayed at Holbrook are a good example of this. They ran 100 sheep, which were mostly 'housed' and were so tame that they could be led around rather than using dogs. For them to see a huge mob of unruly sheep being worked by wildly barking dogs was something of a culture shock, says Alister.

The Holbrook farmstay is located close to Highway 8, only a short distance from Lake Tekapo and its attractions. It was Lesley's idea to start it. Once their children had all left home, she felt a strong need to do something useful. But what? Career opportunities for women on stations are virtually non-existent. A farmstay seemed a way around that. She began them in 1993 and it proved a sensible choice.

It was an overcast May morning when I took coffee with Lesley outside the guests' cottage. She was pleasant and chatty, the same sort of easy company that her husband and brother-in-law were.

The 50-year-old cottage is located about 100 m from the comfortable farmhouse, where the visitors can have their evening meal and breakfast. Featuring a wood-burning stove and heaps of room, the cottage is fully self-contained, and there are a number of restaurants at Tekapo.

Lesley sipped her coffee and commented on the clarity of light here. Many people, she says, when walking at night between the cottage and the farmhouse, can't get over the clearness of the night sky and the abundance of stars. The Mount John International Observatory, perched on a hill (1029 m) above Lake Tekapo, can be visited by arrangement.

A station this size has a lot to offer. Visitors can go and see mobs of sheep on the move. There's also fine rainbow trout fishing on the place, and Lesley has noticed that more and more fishermen are staying with them. Then in summer a wonderful profusion of Russell lupins on the station is something Lesley loves to show off to their guests.

Left: Merinos graze below the Rollesby Range.
Below: Russell lupins on Lake Tekapo's foreshore in late spring.

32 Tasman Downs Station

Hosts: Linda, Bruce and Ian Hayman
Location: Mackenzie Country, eastern shoreline of Lake Pukaki
Address: Tasman Downs Station, Lake Tekapo
Phone: (03) 680-6841
Fax: (03) 680-6851

E-mail: tasdowns@ihug.co.nz
Size: 500 hectares (1100 acres)
Stock: Hereford/Angus cattle
Accommodation: modern 'local' stone homestead, two bedrooms, one private bathroom
Nearest town: Lake Tekapo, 27 km

The raw-boned Mackenzie Country is a high, harsh land of extreme climatic conditions — a huge and virtually treeless basin contained by brutally formed mountains that for much of the year are capped with snow.

I visited Tasman Downs on a day when the Mackenzie Country was seen to best advantage, the end of a long Indian Summer. Pulling up outside the fine stone homestead, I could think of no better place to break a journey between Christchurch and Queenstown than here on the eastern shoreline of Lake Pukaki.

There are 42 properties in the Mackenzie Country that are classed as high country stations. They mostly produce fine Merino wool and in some cases deer and beef.

The property known as Tasman Downs came into being in 1878 when it was sold as a separate unit off Balmoral Station to Mr Newlands. It was made up of 900 hectares of free hold land with a soil cover made from moraine deposits. Later it was transferred to Andrew Cowan, the owner of Tekapo Station, who wintered sheep there. In

1895, the property was sold to Emile Schlapfer who farmed it until 1914 and then sold it to Herbert Elworthy.

Tasman Downs came into the hands of Walter Hayman in 1915. Walter's son Jack and his wife, Lilian, started running the place in 1920. For 23 years she ran the Tasman Downs School which closed in in 1946. When Jack died in 1956, his son, Bruce (an RAF bomber pilot in the Second World War), took over.

These days Bruce is getting on in years and he leaves most of the running of the farm to their 27-year-old son, Ian. It is Ian who conducts the farm tour, which includes visiting the woolshed and yards complex and a trip around the property.

The old homestead eventually vanished when the Lake Pukaki dam was created in the 1950s and later enlarged in the 1970s. By then they had lost more than 300 hectares of their original land. From then on, they ran sheep and cattle until 1995 when the sheep were sold and cattle bought in, along with growing oats and hay as cash crops.

The idea of starting a farmstay goes back 20 years, Linda says. At that time they had some city friends staying. One of them said it was a pity that others couldn't enjoy such a wonderful place and share in such a lovely lifestyle. By then they had built the present-day homestead and Linda realised the possibilities of having paying guests staying with them. How successful an enterprise this has proven to be can be seen by looking at two large maps in the homestead — one a world map and the other of the United States. They are marked to show where their visitors have come from. Many countries are represented and almost every state in the United States. One couple from England have been coming here for a week every year for the last 11 years!

Outdoor activities that can be enjoyed are tramping, fishing and photography. Air flights over Mount Cook National Park can be arranged.

But really it is the overall scenery here that takes your breath away and perhaps there is no finer view available than from the immediate homestead area. Out on the big lawn you look out over Lake Pukaki. Lake Pukaki is 80 sq. km in size. It occupies the lower end of a glaciated valley into which the Tasman River drains. At the head of this valley stands Mount Cook or Aorangi (cloud in the sky). New Zealand's tallest mountain, says Bruce, can be seen from their place around 250 days of the year.

Left: The Tasman Downs homestead looks out over Lake Pukaki.
Below left: Ian handles the farm tours. Here he's seen with Charles the corgi and some working dogs.
Below right: Lake Pukaki and the Ben Ohau Range as seen from Tasman Downs.

33 Omarama Station

Hosts: Beth and Dick Wardell, Annabelle and Richard Subtil
Location: Omarama township
Address: Omarama Station, State Highway 8, Omarama, North Otago
Phone: (03) 438-9821 or (03) 438-9820
Fax: (03) 438-9822
E-mail: subtil@voyager.co.nz
Size: 12,500 hectares (28,000 acres)

Stock: Merino sheep, Angus/Hereford cattle
Accommodation: historic homestead, three bedrooms, one en suite, guests share bathroom
Nearest town: Omarama, walking distance (Originally the station was Omarama, the township came later.)

It was a typical working day in autumn when I had lunch with Dick and Beth Wardell, their stock manager, Guy Martin, and a general hand. While Dick is still involved with the station work, the station is run by their daughter, Annabelle, and their English son-in-law Richard Subtil, who comes from a farming background.

At the moment, the menfolk were working with ewes at the woolshed complex, which dates to 1861. The sheep, having been crutched, would soon be going out with the ewes for 'tupping'. The big event in a ram's year, in other words. They run around 10,000 Merinos here and 1000 head of cross-bred cattle. They also use horses for mustering.

The station was first taken up by Hugh Robison in 1858. It was about 174,000 acres in size and its back country climbed to 1830 m. They would work it in three runs. Typically, a number of owners came and went. In 1884 they were carrying 45,000 sheep. The Wardell brothers, Wilfred and Cecil, started the family's long association with the station when they purchased the homestead block in 1919. Dick and Beth Wardell have been here since 1963.

The Wardells ventured into their farmstay business in 1995. Beth, who does the cooking, much prefers it when their guests, rather than eating out in Omarama, have dinner with them. 'You get to know people so much better when you do that.'

The homestead is delightful. When Beth and Dick moved into it they did some alterations, including the removal of a whole wall of sundried brick which, they found, had been insulated with newspapers dating to 1881.

Guests are welcome to join Dick or either of the station workers during their day to day activities. These include high-country mustering and general sheep and cattle stock work.

Guests can also take advantage of the Omarama Stream that flows through the station. It is widely regarded as one of the finest trout streams in New Zealand. Or they can just revel in a magnificent vista stretching across the Mackenzie Country to Mount Cook itself.

The surrounding district has much to offer too. Omarama — meaning 'place of light' — is two hours' drive from Queenstown. The striking Clay Cliffs can be found here. They rise like fluted columns on the north side of the Ahuriri River and can be reached by motor vehicle. The rare black stilt colony at nearby

Twizel is a popular attraction and the region as a whole is known for its fine trout and land-locked salmon fishing. I personally recommend taking a drive up the Ahuriri River valley.

However, the Omarama district is best known for its ideal conditions for altitude gliding and as a result, two world records for gliding have been set here.

Left: The Omarama homestead.
Above: The historic woolshed.
Right: A striking local attraction are the Clay Cliffs.

34 Fork Farm

Hosts: Lizzie Carruthers and Phill Hunt
Location: Maungawera valley, between Lakes Wanaka and Hawera
Address: Fork Farm, RD2, Wanaka
Phone: (03) 443-1055 or (025) 223-0398
Fax: (03) 443-1170
E-mail: forkfarm@xtra.co.nz

Size: 470 hectares (1100 acres)
Stock: Romney sheep, red deer, Hereford/Angus cattle
Accommodation: Scottish-style homestead dating to 1910, three bedrooms, one private bathroom
Nearest town: Wanaka 9 km

From the high country on Fork Farm it is possible to see Lakes Wanaka and Hawera, both jewels in the magnificent Central Otago landscape. The property itself, consisting of mostly rolling country, is neatly sandwiched between mountain ranges. The overall scenery is stunning. Fork Farm is a great base for any number of outdoor activities as well as being close to Wanaka itself.

The land here was once a part of the 120,000-hectare Wanaka Station, taken up by pioneer runholder Robert Wilkin in about 1858. It was subdivided around 1880. William Kingan appears to have been the first owner of what became Fork Farm.

It was Kingan who commissioned the prominent Dunedin architect, Basil Hooper, to design the present-day stone homestead. He stipulated that it was to be built following traditional Scottish lines. An interesting feature of the homestead is that some of the interior woodwork (kauri and Australian hard woods) was actually recycled from gold dredges abandoned after the Cardrona gold rush petered out in about 1867. The rimu panelling, evident throughout much of the homestead, is especially attractive.

The opening of the homestead dates to 1910. It was a memorable day for the Kingan family who catered for about 150 guests. The homestead drew many flattering comments. So, too, did the farm; it was regarded as one of the finest in the district.

The next owners of Fork Farm were a father and son, K and R Gawn. Things seem to have fallen apart during their ownership since when John Hunt purchased it in 1928, it had mostly reverted to scrub and tussock because of rabbit devastation. But Hunt soon turned things around and today the family still retains Fork Farm. Phill Hunt is the third generation on the place; his parents, Bill and Ruth, are presently retired in Wanaka.

In 1937 the well-known landscape architect, Alfred Buxton, was commissioned to develop a garden which would complement the imposing homestead. A number of exotic trees were planted, among them several oaks, beeches, yews and a large pear tree. Today these splendid trees are an arresting feature of Fork Farm, providing tangible proof of a time when New Zealand was more closely linked with the 'old country'.

Phill and Lizzie Carruthers, a Southland girl who grew up on a farm, have travelled widely. They are young, likeable and progressively minded.

Since the autumn of 1997, they have been welcoming guests to Fork Farm. The couple also provide barbecue lunches, sheepdog

Left: The Fork Farm homestead dates to 1910.
Below: With the Pisa Range forming an arresting background, Lizzie, riding Tom, is shifting some of their cattle.

demonstrations and farm tours for bus tourists. The farm tour lasts two hours and involves hand-feeding deer, and, in season, lambs.

Phill and Lizzie complement each other. They both work actively on the farm. Lizzie does most of the stockwork on the back of her 17-year-old quarter horse, Tom. Lizzie says, 'Basically we just try and be ourselves when people are staying here. We carry on our normal work and if they want to participate in that they are welcome to.'

It was a lovely autumn day when I visited Fork Farm. Taking tea and biscuits outside, I admired the well-tended garden — the homestead and grounds are listed as heritage items in the Queenstown Lakes District Plan. Lizzie told me they are both keen gardeners and they had recently added a large herb garden bordered with lavender.

Phill says that their guests often use Fork Farm's swimming pool and tennis court. Wanaka, he added, is popular in the evenings because of its growing number of fine restaurants.

Daytime outdoor activities that can be enjoyed include skiing at Treble Cone and Cardrona, tramping in Mount Aspiring National Park, launch trips on Lake Wanaka and fly-fishing. Queenstown is an hour's drive away. The most scenic way to get there is via Cardrona and the Crown Range, the highest road in the country (some of which is still unsealed). The Cardrona Hotel, a link with the gold mining days, dates to 1862 and is worth seeing.

Left: **The homestead seen from higher ground.**
Below: **Hard action for Lizzie and Tom and a Hereford bull.**

35 Glenmac Station

Hosts: Kaye and Keith Dennison
Location: Waitaki River valley
Address: Glenmac Farmstay, 7KRD, Oamaru
Phone: (03) 436-0200 or (025) 222-1119
Fax: (03) 436-0202
E-mail: glenmac@xtra.co.nz

Size: 1616 hectares (4000 acres)
Stock: Merino sheep, Hereford cross cattle, horses
Accommodation: roomy, comfortable farmhouse, four bedrooms, share bathroom
Nearest town: Kurow 13 km

A Maori proverb says that if a fantail should alight on your person you will be blessed with good fortune. While the fantail in question did not favour me in such a manner as I sat and talked to Kaye Dennison on the sunny verandah of their cottage, it did flitter about as though it were welcoming me to this high-country station in the Waitaki River valley.

In ancient times, Maori on fishing and hunting forays to the hinterland used this river valley as an easy means of access. They preserved some of what they caught — fish and fowl — for winter use. In bad weather they sought shelter where they could find it. One such place was under rock overhangs near Duntroon (only a short drive from Glenmac). To while away

the time they made drawings on the smooth, soft limestone rock walls of their temporary shelter. These drawings remain today.

Nowadays, much of the Waitaki valley, the boundary between North Otago and South Canterbury, is taken up with stations and farms.

Originally, Glenmac was included within the boundaries of Otekaieke Station. Otekaieke was first taken up by Samuel Pike in 1853. Three years later, William Heywood Dansey purchased the property. Later, it was one of Robert Campbell's many holdings. In 1908 it was sold to the Crown and subdivided. Glenmac dates to that time.

While Kaye Dennison comes from central Canterbury, her husband is a Waitaki man.

They had been farming here for over 20 years when, in 1994, Glenmac came on the market. Eager to take up the challenge of a genuine high-country station they wasted little time in making an offer. They had had a farmstay business on their previous property and continued the same thing here.

They run 4000 Merinos and a small herd of cross-bred cattle. At the time of my visit, the sheep were ranging the high country, which rises to almost 1220 m. They use horses when working cattle. Indeed, the Glenmac stockhorses have proven a hit with many of their visitors. Those who are competent riders can ride without supervision; otherwise someone takes them out. Glenmac is great horse country!

Kaye finds that most of their visitors, once they have been shown to their room and unpacked, are keen to take a walk. Walking, she says, is what most of their overseas guests like doing best.

The Waitaki River is famous for its trout and salmon fishing. The Dennisons work with a local guide if anyone is keen to go fishing for a few hours, a day, or whatever.

Another top attraction is the penguin colony at Oamaru (40 minutes' drive). Since the penguins appear at dusk, dinner is served early that day if anyone is off to see them.

Left: The Glenmac homestead, complete with Sky television.
Above: The Glenmac woolshed.
Below: Kaye and Keith like nothing better than getting out on their stockhorses on their high country.

36 Shortlands Station

Hosts: David and Glenis Crutchley
Location: Maniototo, near Dansey Pass,
Central Otago
Address: Shortlands Station, RD2,
Ranfurly
Phone: (03) 444-9621 or
Free phone: 0800 375-247
Fax: (03) 444-9610
E-mail: d&gcrutchley@xtra.co.nz

Size: 6007 hectares (15,000 acres)
Stock: sheep, cattle
Accommodation: stylish modern
homestead, three guest bedrooms, one
double with en suite. Also: three-
bedroomed farmhouse close to
homestead
Nearest town: Ranfurly 23 km

It was a hot summer's evening when I pulled to a halt at the entrance to Shortlands Station. This was a compelling scene in that part of Otago known as the

Maniototo: the unsealed road heading on towards Dansey Pass itself and the Kakanui Mountains dominating the eastern skyline beyond the main station complex. The landscape was many tones of brown, the sky either vivid or washed-out blue.

I drove on to meet my hosts, David and Glenis Crutchley at their splendid homestead set on lovely grounds. I already knew that the road to Dansey Pass was in effect the northern boundary of Shortlands Station. Before the arrival of the European this route was used by the Maori crossing from North to Central Otago. The pass itself would be named after William Heywood Dansey who, with two others, came by this way in 1855. It would

become a much-used dray and stock track.

The station adjoining Shortlands west of Dansey Pass is Glenshee. It was once a part of Kyeburn Station, the 'big' run in these parts. Still, at 6007 hectares you could hardly class today's Shortlands Station as small. When I arrived at the station they had been working with some of their 12,000 sheep. They run a Merino/Romney flock here and 600 head of cross-bred cattle, too. In summer some of the sheep range to the tops of the Kakanui Mountains.

Interestingly enough, when David's father, Charlie, took on the station in 1946 it only carried 3000 sheep. However, the rabbits numbered in their thousands. David, who has spent his entire life here, can tell you some great stories about rabbits and all sorts of things once he's used to you.

Like his father before him, David is a top sheepdog trialist. He has won and judged New Zealand Championships. When the highly popular television series 'A Dog's Show' was running, he won that twice and took part in nine of the 15 series produced.

As for Glenis, she comes from a farming background in the Maniototo. She is involved with the local community as an enrolled nurse and a St John's Ambulance officer. She rates music and people as her passions. I think you could add gardening, too. It is Glenis who has developed the garden to its high standard — no easy undertaking in a harsh climate.

The Maniototo Basin has very distinct seasons: the fresh green of spring, the hot, dry summers, the gold of autumn and the chill of winter when snow blankets the Kakanui Mountains to low levels and the valley bottoms are covered with frost.

But if farm work is not to your liking, there are other things to do. You can enjoy a four-wheel-drive escorted trip to the top of the Kakanui Mountains or explore the gold workings of the Kyeburn Diggings. If you are a licensed gun holder you can go hunting for pig or deer or night shooting of rabbit or hare can be arranged. As well as going for walks, you can go mountain biking, relax in the pool or exercise on the tennis court. Off-farm activities can include visiting Naseby or Ranfurly or making a day trip to the Styx Basin and visiting the old jail and Styx Hotel. Or there is always lunch at the Dansey Pass Coach Inn.

Above left: The Shortlands Station homestead.
Below left: The mailbox.
Above: David on the Kakanui Mountains looking towards the road to Dansey Pass.

37 Merivale Station

Hosts: Gerald and Mary Goodger and family

Location: West of Lindis Pass, Central Otago

Address: Merivale Station, Lindis Pass, Tarras, Central Otago

Phone: (03) 445-2878

Fax: (03) 445-2878

Size: 3000 hectares (7500 acres)

Stock: sheep, a few cattle

Accommodation: various cottages and units — all self-contained, including outlying musterers' hut. Also three guest rooms (if required) in homestead dating to 1933. Backpacker accommodation; also campervan facilities and tent-sites (with use of homestead facilities)

Nearest town: Cromwell/Wanaka both 50 km

It was a hot mid-afternoon at the Musterers' Backhut on Merivale Station. This single-roomed dwelling is about 8 km from the homestead area. It is, says Gerald Goodger, used on a regular basis by recreational hunters and by some of their guests who fancy a bit of solitude.

I gazed around at the station's hilly terrain, which runs up to about 1070 m. However, there's much higher country beyond the station's boundaries: the Dunstan Mountains to the east, the Pisa Range to the west, and the Saint Bathans Range to the north.

Not a blade of grass stirred out here, not a single sheep or rabbit could be seen. Hot. Still.

Real Central Otago and no mistake. And you can't tell Gerald Goodger a thing about it: he has spent most of his life here on Merivale.

The Merivale story really starts with a tall Scotsman named John McLean who, in 1858, acquired the leasehold rights to 143,500 hectares. This enormous property ran from east of the Lindis Pass almost to Clyde, a distance of over 80 km. At its peak, in the 1870s, they ran 110,000 Merinos on the station.

Subdivision eventually came to Morven Hills. In 1911 James Goodger of Cromwell purchased what became known as Geordie Hill Station. Before he died in the early 1930s, it was split into three: Geordie Hill, Shirlmar and

Merivale. Today, Shirlmar is no longer owned by the Goodger family.

When Gerald Goodger first came to Merivale (named after the Christchurch suburb where his mother was born), he was a baby and today's homestead was only two years old. Later he would become a government deer hunter. He took over running Merivale in 1963; a year later he married his wife, Mary, who came from a farming background in the Mackenzie Country.

At the homestead, Mary Goodger explained that when she came here there was no garden to speak of and no trees for shelter. Today, the garden and an abundance of trees are a welcome sight as you approach the homestead on the kind of sunblasted day I did. The interior of the homestead proved cool and inviting, but on the walls are a number of photographs that prove how hard the winters can be.

I reckon it's a great type of holiday on offer here near the banks of the Lindis River. There's the river itself, a favourite place for the Goodger children when they were growing up, that a lot of their guests find their way to. There's also a swimming pool and a tennis court to take advantage of at Merivale — and plenty of good country fare to tuck into.

What else? Well, there's all the room in the world in which to go hiking. Gerald's keen on hiking. He's also climbed a few mountains, including Mount Cook solo at the age of 61. 'It's not the last time I'll climb it, though,' he says with a confident smile.

Apart from running their farmstay business, Mary likes reading, writing letters, spending long hours in the garden and was until recently heavily involved with local community work. She was the first President of the Child Cancer Society in Central Otago and she is still on the executive.

Naturally you can't spend time at Merivale without having a look around it with Gerald. On my trip, we did eventually see sheep — hardy Merinos that are not hand-fed over winter. We also saw feral goats. They do a great job of controlling the introduced sweet briar, says Gerald.

Of the various types of accommodation on offer at Merivale I like Rose Briar Cottage, which is enclosed in its own garden.

Left: The Merivale homestead.
Below: Rose Briar Cottage.

38 Hiburn Station

Hosts: Claire and Jack Davis
Location: Lowburn, Central Otago
Address: Hiburn Station, Swann Road,
Lowburn, RD2, Cromwell
Phone: (03) 445-1291
Fax: (03) 445-1291
E-mail: hiburn@xtra.co.nz
Size: 404 hectares (1000 acres)
Stock: Merino sheep, red deer
Accommodation: brick farmhouse dating
to early 1960s, two guest bedrooms
Nearest town: Cromwell 10 km

On a lovely day in early spring, I jolted along an unsealed road probing into the foothills of the Pisa Range. A somewhat higgledy-piggledy collection of mailboxes on my right — the Davises' among them — caught my attention. Rural delivery country. Was I really less than an hour's drive from Queenstown International Airport?

Even at this time of the year there was a distinct 'dry' look to the country. This is low-

Left: Lowburn (where Hiburn Station is located) is only a short drive to Cromwell. The Pisa Range as seen in September.
Below left: Across the Clutha River is Cromwell. The distant peaks, seen in August, are the Remarkables.
Right: Jack and Claire Davis with the working dogs gathered about them.

rainfall terrain and as such is an ideal spot for growing fruit, for investing in a vineyard and for raising Merinos.

Presently, I pulled to a halt outside a low-slung, red brick farmhouse. Circa 1962 I would be told; it looked all of its 37 years. Nearby stood a more traditional homestead with corrugated-iron roofing thought to be over 100 years old. Also in sight were a dated woolshed and adjoining sheep yards.

Both Jack and his wife are from Otago; Jack comes from the Rankleburn area where his father farmed, while Claire is from Warrington. After they married, they ran a transport business for 10 years before taking on Hiburn in 1977. They went into farmstays in 1985. Claire says:

'We class ourselves as a real back-country experience. A farmstay to us is not like a normal bed and breakfast. We always take people out on the farm. If Jack has stock work on hand then, and we have visitors arriving, he'll wait until they arrive to do it. That way they can see the dogs working sheep in a real situation.'

The Hiburn sheepdogs are a real treat and just about everyone who comes here loves them. Jack, a noted judge at both local and national sheepdog trials, usually has seven or eight dogs on hand. They include pups learning the ropes, a few oldtimers on the dog pension (which varies from farm to farm), and of course those right up with the play. The dogs, naturally enough, came with us when we went for a look around the farm where Hiburn's stock — some 3000 sheep and 250 deer — all looked in fine fettle.

From high ground there was a stunning panorama of the valley of the Clutha River. Directly across the river were the Dunstan Mountains, while to the north-east and further back rose the snow-covered Saint Bathans Range. Much of this land beyond the Clutha was once a part of the giant-sized Morven Hills Station. The Mount Pisa Run, which Hiburn was once a part of, was also a lot of real estate.

The Pisa Range (1961 m) was initially contained in Robert Wilkin's vast Wanaka Station, which stretched from Makarora almost to Cromwell. The Mount Pisa run was sold to Isodore Loughnan in 1867. In 1881, Howell and Loughnan's Mount Pisa run was listed as 82,044 acres. A stock census carried out in 1891 states they were carrying 34,000 sheep. Meantime the station had increased in size and when it was subdivided into 12 properties in 1920 it was all of 147,000 acres.

Hiburn was the result of a further subdivision in the late 1920s. It would be owned by three generations of the Swann family. They were orchardists. The last Swann on the place sold out in 1970. When the Davises came on the scene seven years later all of the fruit trees had been cleared.

Jack tells me that he never tires of the view from Hiburn's high ground. It was good that he appreciated what he and his wife had here in the valley of the Clutha River and that they were willing to share it, if only for a short time, with people from around the world.

39 Clearburn Station

Hosts: Ian and Margaret Lambeth
Location: near Roxburgh, Central Otago
Address: Clearburn Station, Dalmuir Road, RD2, Roxburgh
Phone: (03) 446-6712
Fax: (03) 446-6774

E-mail: JL.Lambeth@xtra.co.nz
Size: 3228 hectares (7000 acres)
Stock: sheep, cattle, horses
Accommodation: self-contained cottage, twin beds, en suite
Nearest town: Roxburgh 10 km

'There's something about the hills that get to you; we always said we'd come back one day ...' Those words were spoken by Margaret Lambeth on Clearburn Station. Today, the family not only owns the kind of hills Margaret was talking about but also a few high points that can easily be classed as mountains, too.

Margaret comes from Dunedin, and her husband, Ian, hails from Gore. For many years Ian had a career in insurance which took him to the Far East before they ended up in Auckland for 13 years.

In the early 1990s they decided to return to the South Island and those hills they had missed for much too long. What they wanted was a property large enough to support two families — that is, themselves and their son, John, and his family, too.

Eventually it seemed they had found what they were looking for: a large unnamed station near Roxburgh. When Ian and John first looked it over, they liked the high country aspect of it. When John told his mother what they had seen, he said, 'It's got the clearest water in the streams out there you could ever imagine.' It was Margaret who suggested they call it Clearburn ('burn' is a Scottish word for stream). So Ian and Margaret, John and Linda, and their two children, went to live on a genuine high-country station in 1992.

What they named Clearburn appears to have been a part of the huge Moa Flat Estate, which at its peak carried 120,000 sheep. Due to rabbit infestation, that number fell to 45,000. At the height of the rabbit problem, there were as many as 87 men employed as rabbiters. Moa Flat was subdivided after the First World War.

Left: The self-contained cottage at Clearburn Station.
Right: Seen in the autumn, this stone building dates to a time when Clearburn was part of the huge Moa Flat run.
Below right: Heading north from Clearburn towards Alexandra, you pass Butchers Dam. Behind it is the Knobby Range.

The Lambeths started their farmstays in 1996. Being sociable people, it has suited them well as living on a station often means being tied to the place and that does not make for a lively social life. As Margaret says: 'If we can't go out, then maybe we can bring people to us.' This is precisely what has happened here.

Conveniently located between Dunedin and Queenstown, Clearburn had proven popular as a bed and breakfast operation though many people stay longer than one night. An American couple were here for two weeks recently, and that was their second lengthy stay.

The guest accommodation, separate from the main farmhouse, was converted from part of the old shearers' quarters. The view through its sitting room window looks across paddocks to the mountains. Guests take their evening meal with the Lambeths but have breakfast in the cottage. This is a sensible arrangement because the menfolk are often away early in the morning.

Out on the hill range 5500 Merino sheep and 350 Angus/Simmental cattle and a few horses used to muster cattle.

Visitors are encouraged to take part in the day-to-day activities on the place and there's almost always something going on, even if it's only feeding the pigs, hens and a pony. And either Ian or John, work permitting, are only too willing to take guests on a tour to the top of the Benger in a four-wheel-drive vehicle.

Margaret says there are many fine walks to be enjoyed on the place and along the banks of the nearby Clutha River. Within five minutes there are restaurants, a golf course, fishing and many orchards. In season, tours of the orchards can be easily arranged.

40 Mataura Valley Station

Hosts: David, Robyn and John Parker
Location: Northern Southland
Address: Mataura Valley Station, Cainard Road, PO Box 2, Garston, 9660, Southland
Phone: (03) 248-8552
Fax: (03) 248-8552
E-mail: matauravalley@xtra.co.nz

Size: 7680 hectares (19,000 acres)
Stock: sheep, cattle
Accommodation: four guest bedrooms, two king, one double and three single beds; two en suites, one private or guests share bathroom
Nearest town: Garston 17 km and Queenstown 50 km

There are many places of visual and historic significance in this country that, given their location, few people ever get to visit. One place that fits this bill is found in the upper Mataura River country, a geographical location that presents itself differently from most of Southland. Perhaps this is because this country fringes Otago and that the tawny-brown tones of the grassy plains and upon the shoulders of the mountain are more in keeping with the country further north than they are with the usual green aspect of much of Southland.

This is where David, Robyn and John Parker farm on a large scale and also run a farmstay business. The Mataura Station homestead is situated overlooking the river and the view from there of the Eyre Mountains is stunning.

It was a lovely autumn day. David Parker, an English guest and I were high up in the mountains. The Eyre Mountains rising to 1968 m seemed to be almost overhanging us. Most of the station's 300 Hereford cattle were up here in their summer range; some of the cows had calves at heel. Also scattered about the tussocky slopes were some of the Station's 10,000 Merino sheep. Add a few hares to that and a hawk or two and you get the general picture.

The upper Mataura River country will always be linked with the name of Captain John Howell of Riverton. In 1858, with his interests mostly involved with whaling, Howell advised his son-in-law, William Cameron, recently arrived from the Hunter River Country of New South Wales, to search for land beyond Five

Rivers. With a Maori guide, Cameron did just that. At today's Athol he took up land and named his run Glenquoich. He also took up the lease of another run to the north and this he named Bucurochi. In 1860 he transferred his more northern run to his father-in-law. Captain Howell renamed his station after the place of his birth in England — Fairlight, in Sussex.

In the early days, Fairlight had a substantial workforce and they ran cattle rather than sheep due to the demand for beef at Queenstown, where the town's population had mushroomed with the discovery of gold.

The Mataura Valley Station is an ideal place to be based for several days or even longer. With Queenstown's year-round outdoor activities 45 minutes' drive away, and the walking tracks such as the Milford and Routeburn only hours away, staying at the station offers the best of both worlds.

Robyn tells me that they can also arrange aerial tours of the district and they have the advantage of having their own airstrip. You could take a flight from here over Mount Cook or spend a day on Stewart Island — leaving in the morning and returning home in time for

drinks before dinner. The food is also great on the station — lots of traditional fare with the emphasis, says Robyn, on 'fresh organic garden vegetables with salads and fruit'.

Apart from walking and hiking on the station and spending time with the men at work, there are also pigs to feed and, in season, lambs. Then again you might prefer just to take it easy.

Left: The Mataura Valley Station homestead has a view second to none.
Above: David Parker (right) and an English guest. The Mataura River winds down the valley.
Below: The Eyre Mountains.

41 Roselle Farm

Host: Annette Cross
Location: Portobello, Otago Peninsula
Address: Roselle Farm, RD2, Dunedin
Phone: (03) 478-0826
Fax: (03) 478-0852
E-mail: roselle@mail.es.co.nz

Size: 210 hectares (525 acres)
Stock: sheep
Accommodation: self-contained cottage close to main farmhouse — sleeps four, single part bookings only
Nearest town: Dunedin 21 km

Annette Cross enjoys a country lifestyle within easy reach of one of the South Island's major cultural centres, Dunedin. Roselle Farm is a hill country property, typical of those on the peninsula, in that it rises from sea level to about 300 m. The high country affords a splendid view of the other side of the Peninsula including Papanui Inlet. It was from a high point that Annette and I were looking down on the Roselle Farm complex itself. The day was cool, overcast and it had been raining but it didn't matter as the Otago Peninsula, like the West Coast and the Catlins region, has its own special charm and attraction regardless of what Mother Nature comes up with.

Back in the late 1840s when Scotsman, James Seaton, settled here the land was forest-clad from hilltop to almost the water's edge. He cleared enough land to plant a garden and run a few milking cows. Things grew so well here that he was able to sell his produce — including potatoes and strawberries — across the harbour at Port Chalmers or by rowing on to Dunedin.

The Cross family are direct descendants of James Seaton. Brendon Cross, Annette's 25-year-old son, is the fifth generation here. He mostly runs the place, although Annette is not averse to putting in a hard day on the hill or in the woolshed. Brendon is married to Paula, a schoolteacher from Hawke's Bay, and they live in an old farmhouse dwelling in the main complex.

As we looked down on the flat lands around the main working area on the farm, I noticed some black-faced sheep. They were South Suffolk, says Annette, and they had a small stud of 35 animals but their main flock was over 2000. They ran a few cattle, too. Roselle Farm and the surrounding country is ideal for walking.

Dunedin-born Annette is a much-travelled lady. Apart from tramping and the farm itself, she lists her main interests as meeting people and wildlife — especially birds. Annette worked for 14 years at the nearby Royal Albatross Colony at Taiaroa Heads, a year of which was spent working directly with the birds themselves — observing and weighing them and feeding motherless chicks. It was a priceless experience.

At that time there was little bed and breakfast accommodation on the peninsula. Often while at Taiaroa Heads she was asked if she knew of any accommodation in the area. Later, while in England with her two youngest children, they would stay in some of the lovely B&Bs available. On their return they went ahead with starting their own farmstay, converting a 1950s farm cottage into comfortable accommodation.

Today, there is a garden adjacent to the cottage and from its decking you can see the harbour and the grassy flats where the South Suffolk sheep often forage. On the same flats I saw various birds including oyster catchers, paradise ducks and a blue heron. I was told blue herons nest in some nearby macrocarpa trees, which form windbreaks here. The entire Otago

Left: Roselle Farm — the road to Taiaroa Heads can be seen bottom right.
Above: This self-contained cottage is just 21 km from Dunedin.
Below: Near the cottage were South Suffolk sheep.

Peninsula is a birdwatcher's dream come true.

At 30 minutes' drive from Dunedin, Roselle Farm is the perfect escape. It is a farm to enjoy and even closer than Dunedin to a world-famous royal albatross colony and one of the few places in the country where the endangered yellow-eyed penguin can be seen. And then there are all of the other attractions the Otago Peninsula has to offer, such as Larnarch's Castle!

42 Fairview

Hosts: Kaye and Rob French
Location: Waitahuna
Address: Fairview, 75 Waitahuna West
Road, Waitahuna, Otago
Phone: (03) 485-9855
Fax: (03) 485-9855
E-mail: french75@xtra.co.nz

Size: 282 hectares (700 acres)
Stock: sheep
Accommodation: historic two-storey
homestead, three guest bedrooms, guests
share bathroom
Nearest town: Lawrence 12 km

It is the homestead itself that, as you approach Fairview, takes your eye: it stands tall and stately among introduced trees. The Fairview homestead, perched on a high point above the main valley of the Waitahuna River, has been home for Rob and Kaye French since 1972. Rob was born on a farm near here while Kaye comes from Dunedin. They are very proud of their kauri and rimu-built home about which Kaye says:

'Our home was built by Jack McNickle in 1874–75 for his brother-in-law, William Livingston, and his wife, Catherine. William worked on the Victorian diggings in Australia and here at Gabriels Gully before buying Fairview Farm. They had a family of five boys and three girls. The property was sold to the Cranes in 1919.

'We bought the farm in 1973 and renovated it six years later. Most of the verandah had gone and the lean-to kitchen was past its best. The bathroom under the stairs was originally the maids' room. The middle bedroom had never been finished. Our hobbies-cum-playroom was originally their music room. The Livingstons were a musical family and would often play on the top verandah where they could be heard all over Waitahuna.'

At Fairview all of the guest rooms are upstairs. The main bedroom (with double bed) looks out over the side garden. This and the other two bedrooms are all furnished in keeping with an earlier era. The top verandah is a lovely spot to sit in the morning sun.

Almost all of their guests, says Rob, take a farm tour with him. They get about the property in a 1940 four-wheel-drive Ford truck, a big, roomy vehicle of a type that might have been used as an ambulance in the Second World War. The mechanically minded Rob also has some vintage tractors.

Kaye's tastes are somewhat more artistic: she paints, enjoys handcrafts, tends the garden and sometimes helps Rob out on the farm. Some of her paintings, and those of other family members, can be seen by visitors to the homestead.

On the farm, guests can go walking and watch Rob working his sheep. At present, Rob runs nearly 3000 Romneys, a breed well-suited for a climate more prone to rainfall than further north where the Merino rules supreme. There is also a small fishing river on the farm, too.

Away from Fairview, visitors can go horse riding and there are two golf courses less than 10 minutes away. The nearby town of Lawrence, and Gabriels Gully, where gold was discovered in 1861, are both worth poking around. Some of the people who stay at Fairview tend to go further afield. The Catlins is one choice for a day's drive and so is Dunedin, which is only an hour away.

Left: The homestead at Fairview.
Above: Rob and Kaye French with Rob's ex-army truck and a barn dating to the early 1900s.
Below: The pride of the garden is this wonderful old oak tree.

43 Balcairn

Hosts: Helen and Ken Spittle
Location: Hillend, South Otago
Address: Balcairn, Blackburn Road,
Hillend RD2, Balclutha
Phone: (03) 418-1385
Fax: (03) 418-4385
E-mail: balcairn@xtra.co.nz

Size: 202 hectares (500 acres)
Stock: sheep, cross-bred cattle, deer
Accommodation: modern farmhouse, self-contained, two bedrooms, guests share one bathroom
Nearest town: Balclutha 22 km

When I swung off Highway 1 south of Milton, and found myself on the road to Hillend, I thought how appealing the country was here. Essentially, you are following a high ridge above low-lying plains country and the view, running back to mountain ranges, is extensive.

Helen and Ken's property is attractive. Located close to the coast, it rises in elevation to 250 m. Glorious sunsets and sunrises are commonplace here and at night the stars often seem much closer than they really are. Many visitors make sure they draw their bedroom curtains at night so they can see the stars from their beds; it is a lovely way to drift off to sleep after a day on a New Zealand farm.

Ken comes from a Southland farming background, a big, strong type into fishing,

tramping, and, in his earlier days, hunting. While Helen has spent most of her life in Southland, she hails from Central Otago. She enjoys golf and her garden.

They purchased Balcairn four years ago, because they wanted a bigger place than the one they had. The farmstay was already a going business and they simply continued it. Ken says, 'It gives you a whole new outlook on life; it's all been very interesting.'

Their home is a modern, spacious and comfortable dwelling on two levels. From the main sitting-room and balcony you look out over the deer paddocks. There is a feeling of being right among it all.

It appears that Joseph Maitland, who had four sons, took up this land in June 1854. He named his station Hillend. Later, the Begg brothers took it over and in 1890 they were running 15,600 sheep. The Soldiers' Settlement Scheme following the First World War saw the station subdivided and Balcairn dates to that time.

The main attractions on the farm are the deer and working dogs. The deer are used to Ken driving among them and visitors enjoy that very much. They also get a kick out of seeing

Above left: The farmhouse at Balcairn.
Below left: Ken and Helen Spittle; Ken has an arm about Duke, his top working dog.
Above: Early morning at Balcairn.

Duke, the heading dog, show off his stuff with some of their 2600 sheep. Sometimes Ken shows how a sheep is shorn and guests can try shearing for themselves.

My visit was in late autumn. Soon, they would start feeding out until the spring. They would go through 3000 bales of hay plus grain and silage before new growth would bring an end to it. This is a seven-day-a-week chore in all types of weather and everyone is pleased when it's over. They're also pretty self-sufficient on the farm. Helen grows their vegetables: potatoes, broccoli, cabbage, carrots and lettuce.

An interesting day trip that can be made from Balcairn is to the nearby Catlins area. The Catlins forest is regarded as the most important region of native forest on the east coast of New Zealand. The coastal wildlife is fascinating: Hooker's sea lions, fur seals, Hector's dolphins, yellow-eyed penguins, and a wonderful array of seabirds.

44 Glenellen

Hosts: Brigette and Donald Morrison
Location: Waikaka Valley, Southland
Address: Glenellen, RD5, Gore
Phone: (03) 207-1857
Fax: (03) 207-1857
E-mail: rosedale@esi.co.nz
Size: 606 hectares (1500 acres)

Stock: Romney sheep (the Glenellen Romney Stud dates to 1926)
Accommodation: spacious homestead dating to 1954, two bedrooms, one private bathroom
Nearest town: Gore 10 km

There is a soft, gentle look to the rolling, hilly pastures of Glenellen, a rather English-looking rural scene that suits their Romney sheep very well.

There was much movement at Glenellen when I arrived: a locally based shearing gang was hard at work in the three-stand woolshed. Donald Morrison, fifth generation on the place, was busy keeping the ewes up to the shearers with the rather dubious help of huntaway Mac. According to Donald, 'Mac is a general nuisance but he still does a lot of good.' Mac was overly matey, if you know what I mean.

Meanwhile Brigette, Donald's other half, was preparing lunch for the men in the homestead. Just another typical working day on a big Southland farm.

The Glenellen land was once a part of a big run taken up by Alexander McKnab in 1865 who, prior to coming here, had owned a station in Victoria. He named his run Knapdale, after the parish where he was born in Scotland.

There is an interesting story as to how McKnab picked his run. In Australia, James Mackenzie, after whom the Mackenzie Country is named, had worked for him for a time. They were good mates. But when McKnab arrived in Dunedin, Mackenzie was behind bars because of his sheep-stealing exploits. McKnab visited him in jail and explained that he was looking for good land. Mackenzie suggested he take a look at the Mataura River country.

Above: The homestead at Glenellen.
Right: The Willowbank windmill on Glenellen is a local attraction.

McKnab stocked his property with Merinos imported from Australia. By the autumn of 1878 he was running 40,000 sheep. Over the years the property gradually reduced in size and its great days were history. But the woolshed, dating to 1868, still stands near today's Knapdale school.

At present, the Morrison family runs 7000 sheep and crop 400 acres.

English-born Brigette has been running the farmstay venture since 1992. They had so many friends from overseas staying that it seemed natural to turn it into a paying proposition. Brigette loves living on a farm and is often out helping the menfolk as well as keeping their two sons, Lochie and Dirk, in line.

Most of the people who stay with them, including many from North America (purist fly-fishermen), do so because of the world-famous trout fishing the Mataura River provides. There are even trout in the Waikaka Stream (a

Left: Donald Morrison takes a break from working with the shearing gang in the woolshed.

tributary of the Mataura) that flows through the farm. Not long ago, a family from Australia stayed for a week. They liked farm life so much they hardly went anywhere else. One of their children — 11-year-old Jarrod — went out with Donald almost every day. The young fellow revelled in the outdoors lifestyle while for his part, Dad fished on the farm.

When he returned home, Jarrod, as part of a school project, wrote the following:

'Lochie, Dirk, Howie and Brigette are the hosts of the farm we stayed at, they are so nice you would think they are our family. Brigette is a great cook, and I fit her gumboots. Howie works very hard and has long hours. Lochie and Dirk are on school holidays. La La is a very playful lamb, she is hungry at breakfast time mostly. She is a lovely pet to play with.'

Presumably Howie was Donald. What was with the nickname? Brigette laughed. Donald fancied himself as a singer — you know, Howard Morrison? Right!

This farmstay business is a two-way thing and often it's impossible to tell who gets the most enjoyment out of it.

WILLOWBANK WINDMILL & TANK

This windmill was used on the Waikaka branch line for pumping water into the adjacent tank. It stands near the Willowbank Siding of that line which was opened in March 1909 at the urging of local residents and with the aid of their own funds. The railway ran from Gore to Waikaka through agricultural and gold ~ mining country. It was finally closed for economic reasons in 1962. The windmill, built by the Railways Department at its Addington Workshops at the turn of the century, is one of the few remaining in New Zealand.

45 Castlerock Cookhouse

Hosts: David and Julie Thomas
Location: near Lumsden, Southland
Address: Castlerock Cookhouse, Castlerock Road, RD2, Lumsden 9661, Southland
Phone: (03) 248-7435 or (025) 972-465
Fax: (03) 248-7535
E-mail: Cookhse@xtra.co.nz

Size: 1616 hectares (4000 acres)
Stock: sheep, cattle, deer
Accommodation: self-contained cottage converted from station cookhouse dating to 1872, two bedrooms, one double room and one twin room, double sofa bed in living room; single party bookings only
Nearest town: Lumsden 8 km

On a winding, unsealed road out of Lumsden a huge limestone rock arrested my attention. While I had seen a poor black-and-white photograph of it, the reality was more spectacular than I had expected.

Indeed, its steep rock walls, glowing in brilliant sunshine, might have been the ramparts of a medieval European castle. That must have been the way the early owners of Run 181 viewed it too because they named their station Castlerock.

First taken up in 1857, Castlerock was all of 65,000 acres: it stretched from Dipton to Mossburn and was contained by the Oreti River and the Hamilton Burn. At its peak, there were 60 regular hands on the payroll, teams of horses were used for cropping and other

agricultural work and the number of sheep reached 36,000 in 1898–99.

Subdivision began in 1901 but large-scale cutting up of the giant run did not occur until 1935. In that major subdivision the Thomas family purchased the 4000-acre 'Homestead' block; located some 14.5 km from the huge rock monolith that rises 319 m above the surrounding plain. The homestead block came complete with the usual buildings, including the cookhouse. The Castlerock cookhouse is said to be one of the earliest buildings made of concrete in the country. Today the cookhouse is the focal point of David and Julie Thomas's farmstay venture.

It was a fine late winter/early spring day when I drove to the homestead to catch up with Julie and David Thomas. Over coffee, Julie told me that earlier that day four South Devon calves had been born on the place. They ran only South Devon cattle, Julie explained. They had turned from Black Angus cattle in the early 1970s to the more gentle English breed noted for its easy temperament. They now had a registered South Devon stud. In a way, their South Devon cattle had played a part in why they went into the farmstay business.

In Devon in England, while attending conferences on South Devon cattle, they had taken the opportunity of staying in local farmstays and later back home, they spent a night at Olivers in Clyde, where old stone buildings and stables had been converted into a restaurant and guest accommodation. So why not, they said, renovate their old cookhouse for that very purpose. They started work on it in 1992 and two years later it was finished.

The Castlerock Cookhouse is a short walk from the homestead. Surrounded by a picket fence, it faces a big pond. The view from here, looking out over Julie's neat garden, is of the Eyre Mountains. At the edge of the pond a dinghy is tied up for anyone fancying a bit of rowing. The pond is also stocked with brown trout. Fishing, said Julie, was on a catch-and-release basis.

Out on the pond, or close to it, I noticed mallards, pukeko, paradise ducks and a blue heron fishing patiently at the water's edge. Many more bird species were also often seen.

Presently, I caught up with David Thomas at the sheepyards, where he and two regular hands were working with some of the station's 7200 Romney cross-bred sheep. Apart from the sheep, they run 700 cattle and 500 red deer.

The highest point on Castlerock is 365 m. From another high point, Stewart Island can be seen. Down the road, located on another farm, was the rock after which the station was named. Today, Castlerock is more the name of the general farming district than David and Julie's property.

Given its location — 80 km north of Invercargill, 102 km south of Queenstown, and 78 km from Te Anau — the Castlerock Cookhouse is perfectly placed. Many of those who stay are from North America, often trout fishermen from the East Coast. They are likely to spend a week or 10 days at the Cookhouse, using local fishing guides (arranged through Julie) to fish the famous Oreti River. There are also three good golf courses within 15 minutes' drive; and of course many people like to walk or hike on the farmlands.

**Above left: Castlerock Cookhouse — a dream location.
Left: Castlerock (after which today's station and district are named) was more impressive than I had expected.
Below: About as sweet as they come is this South Devon calf.**

46 Crown Lea

Hosts: Florence and John Pine
Location: Te Anau Basin
Address: Crown Lea, Gillespie Road, RD1, Te Anau
Phone: (03) 249-8598 or (025) 227-8366
Fax: (03) 249-8598
E-mail: crownlea@xtra.co.nz
Size: 671 hectares (900 acres)

Stock: Romney sheep, red/wapiti deer, mixed cattle
Accommodation: comfortable homestead, three guest bedrooms, one with en suite, two private bathrooms. Campervans welcomed
Nearest town: Te Anau, 30 minutes

In 1973 Florence and John Pine were able, under the Government Farm Assistance programme, to purchase Crown Lea. It was one of 15 similar-sized properties established in 1962 from what had previously been a 'leasehold' block of mostly unbroken country, red tussock grasslands, scrub and bracken. Red deer and wild pigs were rampant there.

This country was first taken up in 1854 by Freeman Rayney Jackson. His run was contained to the west by the Waiau River, to the east by the Takitimu Mountains, and both north and south by what was described in the lease as 'indefinite' boundaries. The McKay brothers took over the run about 1859. A year later the Gillows brothers purchased the lease for the 25,000 acres of the eastern portion of this run (where Crown Lea is

located) and they named it The Plains. They ran 960 sheep there in the early 1860s.

During the mid-1970s, the Pines, like so many other farming families, needed to diversify to stay afloat. They went into deer farming. In 1989 they branched out even more when they opened up their property for farmstays.

Unless visitors are on too tight a schedule, Florence suggests that two to three days is an

Above: The homestead at Crown Lea looked splendid in the autumn landscape. Right: Florence and John Pine on the highest part of their property. The Takitimu Mountains dominate the background.

ideal length of time to stay. This not only allows guests sufficient time to take full advantage of what the farm has to offer, but it also means the farm can be used as a base for any number of day trips. Within easy distance are Lakes Manapouri and Te Anau and day hikes on the Milford, Kepler and Routeburn tracks can be arranged. Even the Doubtful and Milford Sounds can be visited easily in a day.

On the farm itself, John conducts a relaxed tour of the property in the evening before dinner. He begins by explaining how they do things on the farm, the types of stock they run, and whatever peculiarities they may have. It is not a lengthy talk; most people, John says, have plenty of questions they want answers to.

Crown Lea is clean, attractive country: the stock is well cared for and there are ample shade trees. Given the nature of the land, it is possible to drive to the highest point (430 m) and take in a stunning panorama of the Te Anau Basin. The brooding mountains of Fiordland, to the west, are especially arresting. From another part of the farm Lake Manapouri (20 minutes' drive from here) can be glimpsed.

The sheep at Crown Lea always appeal to overseas visitors, Florence says. During the spring and summer, she always has a few 'orphaned' lambs to look after. They are kept close to the homestead where they are bottle-fed until they can fend for themselves. Guests often enjoy bottle-feeding the demanding little woollies. But the prime attraction here is the deer. John believes this is because deer farming, while widespread in this country, is still novel for those from other places. The star attraction among the deer at the time of my visit was Bambi, an orphaned deer that likes to be made a fuss of.

Left: John finds his red deer fascinating animals to work with.
Below: Bambi, the pet red deer, proved a real delight.

47 Mount Prospect Station

Hosts: Joan and Ross Cockburn
Location: Te Anau Basin
Address: Mount Prospect Station, RD2, Te Anau
Phone: (03) 249-7082
Fax: (03) 249-7085
E-mail: prospect@fiordland.net.nz

Size: 3434 hectares (8500 acres)
Stock: sheep, cattle
Accommodation: large modern homestead, three guest bedrooms, one king and one queen-sized room with en suite bathroom, one twin room with private bathroom
Nearest town: Te Anau 15 minutes

It was midsummer at Mount Prospect Station — peak time for the farmstay business. They were, says Joan Cockburn, booked out until mid-March.

In a country-style short-sleeved shirt and trendy moleskins, Ross Cockburn, taking time out from working with his Simmental cattle, explained that the property had been in the family since 1913. Back then it was known as Mararoa Station, which was all of 40,000 acres. Today's Mount Prospect Station appears to have been an outlying part of that big run.

A Nicholas Clayton took on Mararoa in 1858. It was named after the Mararoa River, which flows between the Livingston and Thomson Mountains and finally merges with the Waiau River some 8 km south-east of the Manapouri village. A year later, Clayton had

380 sheep on his place. It seems that he soon sold out to Low and McGregor, who also failed to make a decent living. By the late 1860s the station was in the hands of land baron Robert Campbell, who had stations in Canterbury and North Otago under his belt. Not satisfied with purchasing Mararoa alone, Campbell added two adjoining stations to it: Mavora and Burwood. This added up to 200,000 acres. His stock returns for 1871 state he was running 94,000 sheep, 29,000 of which were on the Mararoa block. Today, Ross runs 4000 Merino and 3000 Coopworth sheep, and 250 cattle; they have a Simmental stud.

The Mount Prospect homestead dates to 1971. To provide their guests with superior accommodation it was extensively refurbished in 1998 and the end result is immensely

pleasing. Two of the guest rooms, with en suites, look out over the garden to the mountains of Fiordland.

Ross says that a guided activity programme with working dogs, sheep and cattle is always a part of the Mount Prospect package, as are pre-dinner drinks with him and Joan. Ross gives guests his full attention while they are with them. This can mean they stay with him for much of the day as he goes about his normal chores. Ross makes a point to take people to the top of nearby Mount Prospect (over 1000 m). From there is a spectacular view of Lakes Te Anau and Manapouri.

In regards to the menu, Joan always does her best to serve New Zealand lamb and homegrown vegetables.

As well as a guided farm tour and farm activities, there are farm and bush tracks and plenty of fishing opportunities on Mount Prospect. Scenic helicopter flights are available by arrangement. Attractions within driving distance include Milford and Doubtful Sounds and the Fiordland National Park — as well as possibilities for sea kayaking, diving, sailing and tramping.

Left and above: The Mount Prospect Station homestead.
Left: Joan and Ross Cockburn relax in the sun.

Within driving distance of Mount Prospect Station, Milford Sound is a favourite spot for people touring the deep south.

48 Rarakau Station

Hosts: Sheryll and Thomas Bowen
Location: adjacent to Fiordland, Southland
Address: Rarakau Station, Papatotara
Coast Road, Bluecliffs Beach, RD1,
PO Box 23, Tuatapere
Phone: (03) 225-8192 or (025) 448-510
Fax: (03) 225-8192
E-mail: rarakau@southnet.co.nz
Size: 1300 hectares (3000 acres)

Stock: cross-bred cattle, sheep, deer,
horses
Accommodation: modern farmhouse, one
bedroom, one double bed, one single bed
(cot available), family share bathroom.
Also a unit that sleeps up to 24 people
and a dining/amenities block with
meeting and cooking facilities
Nearest town: Tuatapere 20 km

There is a definite feel of the 'last frontier' about Rarakau Station. It is tucked away on the coast some 120 km south of Te Anau, the very last property before the Fiordland wilderness takes over.

Rarakau was originally granted to Sheryll's ancestors in 1906 under the South Island Landless Native Act. It was incorporated in 1967, and its running was taken over by the Maori Affairs Department for many years. Today, it is owned by over 700 Maori shareholders — including Sheryll. Sheryll and Thomas have been running it since 1997.

Even today (apart from some small areas cleared for farming) this is 'unbroken' country and therein lies its main attraction.

Much of Rarakau is clad with native forest. It is a wonderful place to see such trees as rimu, totara, rata, matai, and kahikatea, the tallest forest tree of them all. A diversity of birdlife thrives in the forest around the farmhouse. I heard a number of birds while I was there and they are very vocal in the early mornings.

Red deer and wild pig abound on the station

and Thomas has shown many people just what a deer looks like in the wild. All of the deer they have — contained in a big, well-sheltered enclosure near the farmhouse — have been captured in the immediate area. Some of them are now tame enough to eat out of your hand.

Another appealing aspect of Rarakau Station is that over 7 km of its southern boundary is Bluecliffs Beach. The narrow strip of sand, littered with driftwood and shingle, has a 'wild' look about it as it curves out to the far headland within Fiordland itself. On that skyline is the forest-clad Hump Ridge (1067 m). The Hump Ridge is presently being developed as a major walking track. Rarakau Station is the gateway to the South Coast's tracks.

On the far foreshore, below that range, are the remains of what was once a bustling industrial centre named Port Craig. There was a large settlement there and a big timber-mill. But all that ended in the late 1920s and fell apart in the Depression of the 1930s.

There is good fishing to be had off Bluecliffs Beach, especially blue cod and flounder. Out in Te Waewae Bay it is sometimes possible to see Hector's dolphins or migrating muttonbirds flying low over the often violent waters.

Thomas is a keen hunter and loves the outdoors. Game hunting for wild deer and pigs can be arranged or Thomas is happy to show you around the farm. He can also be

easily convinced to play the guitar, anytime!

Sheryll enjoys gardening, photography, cooking — including making homemade bread, preserves and curries — and of course her animals. They enjoy entertaining, and love sharing their knowledge of the area. They offer guests a friendly, relaxed household and guests are free to join the family for meals and activities, and to make themselves at home. Their two children, Luke and Emma, are typical active young children and enjoy having visitors as much as their parents do.

Left: The farmhouse is basic but cosy and is in keeping with its surroundings.
Above: Sheryll Bowen and her daughter, Emma, with Arnie the pet Perendale sheep.
Below: Some of the station's southern boundary is this wild coastline, which sweeps around to old Port Craig.

49 Greenwood

Hosts: Alan and Helen-May Burgess
Location: the Catlins
Address: Greenwood, Purakaunui Falls Road, Owaka, South Otago
Phone: (03) 415-8259 (if no reply, ring after 6 pm) or (025) 384-538
Fax: (03) 415-8259
E-mail: greenwoodfarm@xtra.co.nz

Size: 808 hectares (2000 acres)
Stock: sheep, cattle, deer
Accommodation: homestead dating to 1920s, three bedrooms, one queen, three single, one en suite. Campervans welcome. Also available a self-contained house at Papatowai Beach (sleeps eight)
Nearest town: Owaka 14 km

Through a lingering tapestry of mist the 200 m cliffs were suddenly before and, seemingly, right below me. It was reason enough to step back sharply and to flash a somewhat rueful look at my grinning host, Alan Burgess. The air was filled not only with the sound of the sea but also the cries of seabirds. The wind's cutting breath, driving in relentlessly from the south, was cold enough to freeze hands and to bring sudden tears to one's eyes.

I was midway through a farm tour on what was the second most southerly property I'd visit while working on this book. That good-natured Alan would also take me to where yellow-eyed penguins were nesting was another surprising aspect of my visit to Greenwood in the intriguing Catlins district.

Alan Burgess has spent all of his working life on Greenwood, where he winters 3250 Romney sheep, 350 Hereford/Angus cross-bred cattle, and 200 red deer. It is attractive country dotted with stands of native timber.

Over the years the property has increased in size. It started out in 1906 as a 150-acre bush block taken up by William Joseph Burgess, Alan's grandfather. He felled the timber, spread grass seed by hand over the cleared ground, and ran a few milking cows. In the nearby sea, fish were plentiful and wild pigs — meat on-the-hoof — were rampant.

Later, Normand ('Chum') Burgess, Alan's father, made enough money out of possum skins that he was able to purchase land adjoining the farm. Later still, Alan himself snapped up more land and today Greenwood is one of the bigger land holdings in the district. His two sons, Brett and Karl, also farm nearby.

Alan and Helen-May Burgess have been running their farmstay business for 15 years. It all started because Alan would often meet hikers and bikers on the road and, as accommodation used to be hard to find anywhere in the Catlins, he would offer them a bed for the night. It became a regular thing for Helen-May, a schoolteacher at Owaka, to come home and find a strange pack or packs sitting on the verandah and a couple of strangers having a cup of tea with Alan in the kitchen.

Initially, they offered basic backpacker accommodation; later, realising the potential of what they had to offer, they opened up their home as a farmstay. The homestead, dating to the 1920s, features extensive use of local rimu

Left: The Greenwood homestead.
Below: Out of Owaka is Catlins Lake. The road to Greenwood passes the farm buildings across the lake.

and has a warm, homely feel. I stayed in a separate wing with a spacious bedroom, looking out over farmlands, a separate living room, and adjacent bathroom. At the time of my visit, the cows were calving, and, because of a sudden cold snap the winter feed-out routine, even though it was spring, was still going on.

Greenwood is great for using as a base for exploration of the Catlins. There is something of a 'last frontier' about this region from where, alas, many families have drifted away over the years because of a lack of work. Today, as you drive out past Catlins Lake en route to Greenwood, it is difficult to imagine that back in the 1870s this was among the busiest of ports in the country.

The station itself is ideally suited for easy walks or more strenuous hikes. There is even talk about opening up a coastal walk here, something similar to the one on Banks Peninsula. Personally, I loved the wild headland country and found the yellow-eyed penguins a delight. Another appealing aspect of Greenwood, perhaps the highlight for some who visit there, are the famous Purakaunui Falls. They are an easy stroll from the homestead. A far-sighted William Joseph Burgess actually gave the forested block of land, where the falls are to be found, to the Government.

50 Greenbush

Hosts: Ann and Donald McKenzie
Location: Fortrose
Address: Greenbush, 298 Fortrose-Otara Road, RD5, Invercargill
Phone: (03) 246-9506 or (025) 239-5196
Fax: (03) 246-9506
E-mail: greenbush@nzhomestay.co.nz

Size: 404 hectares (1000 acres)
Stock: sheep, cattle
Accommodation: 1920s homestead set in lovely grounds, three guest bedrooms, one double, four single; guests share bathroom
Nearest town: Invercargill 50 km

As Lewood out of Okaihau was the most northerly of all the farmstays I would visit, then, by the same token, the last property I called in at, Greenbush was the most southerly.

My first impression of Greenbush, on a blazing hot afternoon, was of a beautiful garden and grounds and, set among them, an appealing homestead. Much was happening there when I arrived. Ann McKenzie (heaps of good-natured fun) was expecting some guests from overseas and her husband, Donald, was at the woolshed and yards complex where five-year-old Coopworth ewes were being loaded into a huge stock truck. They were off to Canterbury for breeding purposes. Also, visitors were admiring the garden which, as a part of Southland's Festival of Gardens project, was open to the public.

Greenbush was taken up by Kenneth and Catherine McKenzie in 1865. It was then a 50-acre bush block. They built a home, worked hard, and it paid off because their three sons owned adjoining farms so that collectively, the family appears to have owned around 3000 acres.

In 1924 the present homestead was built by the second Kenneth McKenzie and the old building was pulled down. Then in 1940, Donald's father and mother (also named Ann) were married and moved into the homestead. About that time Ann was given a young kauri tree. This tree was pointed out by today's Ann McKenzie. It is considered to be the oldest kauri tree in Southland. Other trees in the garden include elms, Californian redwoods, golden ash and black or Southland beech.

A searing hot wind, most un-Southland-like, was keeping Don McKenzie company as we drove around the farm. On pasture formed on sandhills, sheep appeared to be doing very well. They run about 4000 Coopworth ewes here and a few beef cattle. An appealing aspect of Greenbush is that some 2 km of it is bounded by the coastline. From near there, looking across Foveaux Strait, Stewart Island is clearly visible. Some of the sunsets over the island, says Don, are just wonderful.

Perhaps the most striking feature of the farm is a large natural lake named Lake Vincent. The lake is home to Canada geese, black swans and paradise ducks. The lake is included in a designated walk from the homestead itself.

Donald McKenzie has lived here all of his life, and he farms the property with the eldest of their three sons, Scott. Another son farms locally, and Don's brother also has a farm in the district. Don likes fishing. They had fresh blue cod on the menu that night. Canterbury-born Ann enjoys spinning, meeting people and spends a lot of time in her garden.

Fortrose, where Greenbush is located, can be seen as the gateway to the Catlins. Within a short distance of Greenbush is Waipapa Point.

I found Waipapa Point fascinating, with its grassy sandhills and a curving beach of golden sand. Here on the reef the SS *Tararua* sank with a loss of 131 lives in 1881. The wooden lighthouse that stands here now dates to 1884 — three years after the tragedy. Down on the beach itself, near the reef, I spotted two huge sea lions. Wisely, I kept my distance. There was also a profusion of birds there, too, and a fisherman, on nearby rocks, was hauling in one big blue cod after another.

Left: The homestead at Greenbush bathed in February sunshine.
Above right: Donald McKenzie and some of the Coopworth ewes about to leave the property.
Right: The natural lake, and stock-dotted pastures at Greenbush. Some of the farm buildings can be seen through the gap in the trees, to the left of the treeline.

By the Same Author

New Zealand Non-fiction
Pack and Rifle
Hunter by Profession
Backblocks
The Deer Hunters
Seasons of a Hunter
The Hunting Breed
On Target
The Wild Pig in New Zealand
The Golden Years of Hunting in
   New Zealand
The Golden Years of Fishing in
   New Zealand
New Zealand: Hunters' Paradise
Holden on Hunting
The Deerstalkers
A Guide to Hunting in New Zealand
The Hunting Experience
Hunt South
Wild Game
More Holden on Hunting
Fall Muster
On the Routeburn Track
In Search of the Wild Pig
Station Country
Always Another Hill
Wild Boar
Holden's New Zealand Venison
Cookbook
Station Country II
Pack and Rifle (1995 edition)
Great Hunting Yarns
The Way of a Hunter
Station Country III
New Zealand Hunter
A Backcountry Journey
Walking the Routeburn Track
The Milford Track Adventure
Walking the Abel Tasman Coast Track

Young Adult Fiction
Fawn
Stag
White Patch
Razorback

Children's Fiction
Lucy's Bear

Children's Non-fiction
Sheep Station

Australian Non-fiction
Outdoors in Australia
Along the Dingo Fence
Crocodile
Wild Pig in Australia